FINDING ELIZABETH

YOUR STORY UNFOLDS

To the moon,
I tell my secrets and wait for the sun to help me grow,
for I am only a rose covered in thorns.

Prologue

My life took a tumble, I think all lives do; but I never expected to experience such loss at sixteen. Most people at that age receive their first car others get one heck of a sweet sixteen celebration; I was shoved into adulthood, and into realms I had no idea existed. Seeing my mother helpless the day my father died broke me.
I saw them. Moving the sofas, the display cabinet, and the coffee table to the bedroom; all vintage left by my grandparents. They pushed the other furniture against the wall, creating more space for people to come in and mourn.
Why are they doing this? I thought,
My father is still at the hospital. I told him he was going to be fine, and he nodded. I saw him crying, maybe it was because he was in pain... it is without question not because he was leaving. I could hear conversations in my head as I was sitting outside, watching people walking in, neighbors, friends of my fathers, relatives... they all walked in.
Go away;
my screams were not as loud as I wanted them to be. My mouth was sealed shut, I could not open it even if I wanted to; they would not understand the fight that was brewing within me.

Where were you all when my father was sick?
Where were you when we did not have food, where were you?
A barrage of questions flooded my mind as they looked at me, eyes drooping, tears gushing out. "I'm sorry Lizzy for your loss," they consoled me.
No! No! No! He is not gone; he is just at the hospital he is coming back. My tears gushed down my cheeks. I could only hear what I wanted to say, my mouth did not move. I ignored them, sat with my arms folded across my chest.
Run! Then I heard a voice, as clear as day. *Run. get out of here!*
I had the sudden urge to bolt, run and run until I could not run anymore. I wanted to go to the hospital, I wanted to go find him and tell him that people were gathering, saying that he was gone. I wanted to prove to everyone that my father was still there. I stared into the dark, the stars did not twinkle, the moon was hiding...
God was hiding from me. With conviction, He knew what he had done.
I was jolted from my trance by someone crying, then another and another; a chorus of weeping and constant wailing.
Please stop! None of them stopped, they could not hear me. They were hurting me with all the lies they came with. I was certain that it was some kind of evil joke played on me to satisfy their sadistic pleasures. *How could they just accept it? How?*

I was cheated, I prayed for him to heal but he left.
We had plans, he was going to get ten million one day and change our lives.

"One day my kids, I will get ten million and our lives will change; I promise you" my father would say while we sat enjoying a movie.
"I will buy my daughter a mini cooper, just her because your mother doesn't want to learn how to drive." He would say to my mother, trying to annoy her for a laugh.
We had plans, and down the drain, they went.

I remember looking up to the sky, looking for answers I guess, maybe; something that would make sense of everything. I thought I would see his face, sitting amongst the mourners and scream out I'M BACK! Was it too much to ask for? After his funeral, I waited for him to return, *it's not funny anymore dad, come back,* I thought. I waited to hear him say "You people, I'm hungry what did you cook?" while busting into the doorway.
Now I was stuck with a gift I did not want and a wound in my heart that I was not sure was ever going to heal. Lost, confused, and broken.
As I walk down the passage in our house, I recall standing beside him in the passage looking at mom, making fire through the window. He laughed at her as she poured oil on the wet firewood; surely a very unconventional and snobbish way of making fire but we needed to eat, and there was no electricity. He pulled me close to him and said, *"You guys will struggle when I'm no longer here. You can't even make fire?"* I wonder, DID HE KNOW. Did he know that he was leaving?

Time heals SOME wounds...
It's just you, and me, mommy. JUST YOU AND ME NOW...

Chapter 1

April 11 1994 must have been a bittersweet moment for my parents; they had my birth to celebrate and my sister's death to accept. My mother says that my twin sister was born sick; with an illness still do not quite know or understand, since my mother does not talk much about her; except that we were identical twins. I remember the day I found out that I was a twin, I was so excited to be different from almost everyone I knew; it was during one of my snooping escapades I did to feed my curiosity, I came across a piece of paper that had my mother's name and the name of the hospital I was born in. I must have been around eight or nine, when I realized there was more to the dreams that visited me almost every night. Before knowing about her, I would dream of a person with a precise splitting image of mine coming to my rescue whenever I was in danger. Knowing about her gave me some sort of comfort; I did not know I needed. I had always been one to bottle up my emotions; it must have been because I had never felt like part of a clan, be it at school, or at home or it could have been one of the traits I inherited from my mother.

I had an average childhood, filled with vivid imaginations where I confided in my stuffed toy bunny. He was grey with huge ears that had a tinge of pink that matched his nose and mouth. He looked dapper in his blue dungaree that was sown onto his body. Out of my eleven stuffed toys, Bunny was my favorite. He knew about my fears, dreams and everything that made me happy. We used to hide under the covers at bedtime, I would tell him all I wanted to be in future, and as weird as it may sound, he would talk back. I know it sounds crazy but Bunny used to give the best ideas_ well good enough for a child. Bunny was my best friend, as sad as it may compresence, I was okay with that. It kept me out of trouble and maybe made me a focused little human. I was brought up in a middle-class family, my father a self-employed auto mechanic and my mother a stay at home mom who always made sure I had everything that I ever wanted. My grandfather was a retired ZUPCO employee and used to entice me with loads of stories from the time he worked in Bulawayo until the relocation to Gweru. Simpson Taderera, my grandfather had been widowed a year before I was born, so I never met my grandmother. He was a lover of fine things; he only drank the best quality of whiskey with a dash of milk. I always wondered what he enjoyed from that golden liquid. My fondest memory of him is the time I got into trouble for redecorating the outside wall with mud and he came to my rescue. I was about six then; I got away with scrubbing the wall clean, even though he was not impressed with my attempt at being Picasso, I was rewarded with an apple. The bond between him and me might have been brought by the fact that he named me, I am sure my mother and father had a bunch of names to give my twin sister and me but it was without doubt not their place to do so. He gave me his wife's name, Elizabeth; he must have missed his wife and this, was one of the ways he knew of honoring her.

My seclusive nature throughout school earned me the snob title. I am sure some of my classmates saw me as a teacher's pet, because I sure did feel like one. I could not help but be punctual with school assignments and made sure that I was always on the right side of the law. I hated being little miss perfect but I could not help myself. I became an outsider amongst my peers and I was left out on inside jokes. I was never bullied, at least not in an extreme way that would have traumatized me, but there was this one time I was in grade one where a classmate of mine thought it would be funny to dip her hands in my lunch box. I was disgusted; I threw away the food and told my mother as soon as I got home. I remember my mother rushing to the market where my classmate's mother had a vegetable stall and gave her a mouthful on the matter.
My mother always had my back, and we would only tell my father if the issue had escalated beyond our control; just like when I was in high school and my geography teacher gave me a slap after a misunderstanding with the whole class. I was not the only one who was slapped but I was the sole pupil to suffer the aftermath of what felt like a fifty-pound hammer swerved right across my face. leaving a feeling of what felt like my brain hitting back and forth across the skull, and in the excruciating process, carrying my eyeballs right into my eardrums. It was too hard to bear even for a few fleeting seconds._ that saw my father marching into the headmaster's office. I recall being very scared of going back to school the next day.
My parents gave me the freedom to dream, I would change my ambitions simply because I felt I did not want to be what I had chosen to be in the first place. There was a time I wanted to be like my grandmother, a nurse. The black and white photographs in my grandfather's album bred so much curiosity that I wanted to know more about her. I would snoop around in my grandfather's room looking for secret treasures that might have belonged to her. I admired my grandmother's beauty, I would try to pick out similarities between the two of us, and I found a mole under my left eye that she also had. This somehow strengthened the connection I already felt with her.

Spirituality played a role in my upbringing and so did tradition. My family used to take part in some customs that were very fascinating to an open-minded child like myself. My first experience with an African custom was when my grandfather held a ceremony in honor of my grandmother. They call it *Kurova guva*, this ceremony is usually done a year after the death of a family member; I wonder why they waited this long because my grandfather held it when I was in primary school, years had already passed. I remember watching my grandmother's sisters making preparations and brewing the beer that was meant for the event. I became fascinated with tradition, though some of the things scared me I wanted to learn more, but it was only until I discovered that I had some sort of spiritual gift that was slowly growing within me. It started as dreams and premonitions; at first, my parents thought that I had a wild imagination and did not always take me seriously, until one day when a traditional healer told them about a gift that was hiding in me. I never used to tell my school friends about the events I attended and the premonitions I used to have I was already considered a weirdo and this was going to be the icing on the cake. Secretly I would learn about these customs and create what they called a *"musalad"* façade. I had already earned the snob title so it was easy to be one.

The spiritual awakening used to scare me, especially when the dreams seemed to be happening in reality. Like this one dream, where I dreamt of a woman weeping in my room, her sniffles where so realistic and it felt as if I had my eyes open at one point. I recall her wailing and shaking the bed and it felt as though an earthquake was taking place, then out of the blue, a monitor lizard waltzed in and attempted to pull me out of my bed, I felt the grip of its mouth on my ankle tightening with each struggling movement I made. I remember closing my eyes and praying, then there is a choral like singing, when I opened my eyes, my sight lay on the window. Through the window, I saw three figures dressed in white and they looked like they were in the clouds, they continued singing and as they sang it made the monitor lizard restless and it loosened its grip and the woman who was crying screamed as she went away and there was silence. The singing, the crying, the growling stopped; it was dead silent. The visions and dreams became a part of me throughout my life, some days worse than most days until one day when the voices started.

Sometimes I think I have some connection with death, because for a long time I have been able to sense the angel of death whenever he was near. I feel like this connection was made when I was born; losing my twin sister might have not had a strong effect on me physically but it might have done so spiritually. My first known encounter with death came sometime in 2005, a Saturday one of the two days I was allowed to watch TV early in the morning. I could only watch TV at this time because my mother and grandfather would be glued to it when it was soccer time. I never liked soccer, I still do not; the game confuses me even though I have been given lessons countless times. On this particular Saturday morning, I woke up early to catch my regular cartoon the Tom and Jerry kids show; I heard a noise coming from my grandfather's room. It sounded like he was struggling to breathe, I remember walking up to his door and placing my ear, trying to listen through it. The noise grew restless; I ran to my parents' room and told them that I thought something was wrong with Sekuru.

They told me not to disturb him and give him time to rest; you see sekuru had been ill for a long time and with my record of nagging him, my parents thought that was one of those days. I went back to my TV show feeling a bit disturbed; my gut told me that something was wrong. I listened through the door again and I heard him gasping for air, frantically I dashed back to my parents' room and this time I dragged my father out of bed; upon hearing the ruckus our tenant at that time sekuru Mombe got out of his room and went together with my father in my sekuru's room. They found him lying in bed motionless and gasping for air. I was sent to the living room and my father called the ambulance while sekuru Mombe tried to perform first aid. When the paramedics came and gave him the treatment he needed he was better. I remember my heart pounding in my chest; I could feel a heavy eerie spirit hovering around, but could not tell what it was. Sekuru was later taken to the hospital in my father's car, this was days after the incident; he never liked the ambulance; he claimed that if he went to the hospital in it, he would never return. I guess he was wrong, the angel of death took him, despite the type of vehicle, he went to the hospital with, and I was robbed one person that fueled my curiosity.

As it would seem being a teenager was not as amazing as it sounded. My spiritual gift had been growing and evolving, I had started to hear voices, and they came with nothing but bad news.

28 June 2011 marked the worst day of my life. The night when my father's illness showed fatal signs, we did not have electricity; the power company had gone round in our area cutting off electricity for those who had not paid. My father started heaving in deep pain; I fumbled for the phone to turn the torch on while my mother fumbled for some water. He took a sip of the water, and then started telling us how he would love for his intestines to be turned upside down. We laughed, my mom asked him,

"*How can that be possible love?*" he kept quiet and did not respond. I wiped his forehead with my palm, his temperature was lower than earlier, and I thought it was because he was getting better. I did not put much thought to it. He then said he could not feel his feet, my mother made him sit on the bed and I knelt in front of him and held his feet in my hands, they were cold. I prayed more than I had ever prayed before in my life trying not to pay any attention to the temperature and rubbing them with my hands to bring the warmth back. I begged God with my tears flowing. Suddenly, I heard a voice speaking to me.

"*Your God will not hear you; your father's time has come.*" I opened my eyes and looked around to see who had spoken to me, my mother was still deep in prayer, and my father was just sitting, perhaps listening to our continuous rumblings. I noticed that neither my mother nor father spoke so I rebuked the voice, I shouted at the top of my lungs telling the voice that he was wrong. The voice laughed at me and mocked my requests to God. I cried asking God to hear my prayers, but the voice grew louder than my cries.

Memories of my father sleeping on the stretcher bed in the ambulance with his tears flowing down his face sometimes send me to a dark place; one filled with anger and hate and most times, I feel as though my father's departure happened in haste. It feels as if I had been robbed off my childhood and been forced to grow up. There was the "gift" that had been thrown onto my lap, the nightmares, and night terrors that came with it; though I was getting used to it all, I now had to deal with losing the one person who was my hero. I knew my father as a strong person the one time I saw him at his weakest was when he was on the stretcher in an ambulance. I tried to be strong for him when I saw him shedding tears, I hid mine and wiped his away; I told him everything was going to be fine; then everything came spiraling down and it left me broken.

Chapter 2

My father was pretty much a family oriented. He made sure that I had all I wanted, even the little things like pocket money until the alcohol is forcing him to sleep so he may go sober again... He loved to joke around, and when drunk, his humor would go all out for hours. When he was sober, he would have us moving furniture around and then leave my mom and me to finish off what he had started while he went out with his friends. He was always working_ a mechanic who was very passionate about cars. I admired that about him and for someone who still had to figure out what I wanted to be; he was the perfect blue print. His absence did not dawn on me until his passing, that is when I realized that I spent most of my childhood with him away, it kinder made the pain of losing him become worse. I think I never realized my father's absence because of the presence of my mother or maybe because of the love he showered me whenever he was around. I remember being his spanner girl when he brought some work home, thanks to him I can tell the difference between a shifting spanner and a screwdriver. He was tall and had a slim stature. My mom would make fun of him whenever he walked, he would slouch as if he wanted to hide his real height. He was light in complexion, my mother always said that his hazel eyes made people think he was coloured.

Before his demise, I recall my father asking me about my exams, he asked me what I wanted to do after I was done with them. We were sitting outside under the mango tree; he was looking better than the previous days and we all thought he was healing. We sat for hours talking about everything and anything that we could think of. I did not tell him about the voices that I was hearing when I was alone; I had already scared them with the nightmare I had. That day my father took one of his screwdrivers and carved some writings on the tree trunk. It read Lizzy, daddy and mommy forever and he drew a heart shape over it. I looked at him and he had a proud look on his face after our lengthy conversation.

Losing him changed me, I loathed the gods and everything spiritual; I was hurt by him. I wondered why I even bothered praying to him. I told myself there was no God. The hate grew worse as I saw my father leave home lying in a coffin. I was shattered and wanted to die too, thought maybe if I did, I would not feel the pain that was stirring in my heart. It felt like a huge pin was stuck in my heart and a hammer was being used to wedge it in deeper. I thought it was the end of my life. I wondered what I had done wrong to deserve such fate. I had always imagined my father walking me down the aisle someday just like in the movie. I have always been a prayerful young girl, taught by my mother, but when the sandstorm hit my home; I felt like He had forsaken me. I found no other reason to pray. God had taken away the one person that made our family complete. Losing him brought about an indescribable pain as I watched a world that I knew crumble, forecasting an uncertain future. Thorns grew creating a wall that hid all the hurt I felt inside of me.

It became clear that I had the ability to sense death's presence from an early age; I just did not know. Being informed about death in the family was not the first time as it would seem, before my father, I recall it happened when I was about to lose both of my puppies. When the first pup Jessie was about to die, she came to me in my dreams and she spoke to me, thanking me for being a great friend to her and she told me she was leaving. I remember waking up and hearing my other pup yelping just to find out that Jessie had died that night. They were a present from my dad; he loved dogs and thought it would be great if I had my own. Jessie was very tiny when she came to me, she was a cute Doberman with a huge scar on her neck; apparently her previous owner had whacked her with a burning stick. I fell in love with her the first time I met her, and gave her a bowl filled with milk not knowing that I was over feeding her; the poor pup had trouble sleeping. Excitement kept me up that night and the nights that followed. As she grew and gained her strength, we changed her meal and added sadza to the milk and alternated the milk with soup from meat. She loved sadza and milk; I could tell that by the way she would jump up and down with excitement. Jessie became Bunny's replacement; I would talk to her about everything that happened at school and what deeply desired. Then came Spike, he looked exactly like the dog my father had when he was a young boy hence the name. He was a Great Dane and exactly Scooby Doo's look alike, he was not as gentle as Jessie was; he was a bit rough even when he walked, knocking down everything in his way including his bowl with sadza and milk, except when it had meat soup; he loved it with meat soup and bones. It was funny how I felt like the dogs had some kind of human nature within them; whenever I played with them I felt like they were humans trapped in the dogs. As crazy as it may sound I felt I had real friends and losing them made me think that life was just an illusion; losing my father didn't change this perspective.

I wish I were more like my mother, her ability to forgive surpasses mine. I failed to understand how she was able to pray after everything God had done to us. Anger brewed in me like a volcano waiting to erupt; like her, I bottled up my pain. I would plaster a smile on my face during the day and drown my pillow with tears at night. Grappling my father's passing proved to be difficult. I needed answers to questions that were in my head. I did not understand why God did not answer me, or why he did not show up when I called him. My mother tried to get me to pray, I could not bring myself to talk to Him. I felt like he was a deceitful god, preying on our naïve selves to gain worship while he promised us 'happiness' that never came.

A part of me thought that my father had been murdered, attacked in the unchartered spiritual world by a witch or an evil relative that casted an evil eye on my family. I started gathering facts leading to my father's death. The first clue was the weird phone call he got and we only heard crying on the other end. My father had just returned from South Africa, and we were sitting in the living room talking enjoying ourselves. His phone rang, it was an unknown number, and when he answered the person on the other line was crying screaming out his name. The voice resembled that of my grandmother (his mother's sister) who had passed on. When my father hung up the call, we tried calling everyone we thought could have called or have a voice that was similar to hers. A week later, he fell sick and died. I was certain that call was behind everything. The other clue I thought of was the 'fight' between my parents and our neighbor. Something that had never happened before; our neighbor's daughter-in-law had reported us to the electricity supplier and told them about our illegal electricity connection that my father had done. I heard the woman tell them, and the supplier cut our connection. My father was furious, they had a word brawl, and out of that, some bad words were said. I was certain that some negative energy was let loose and was a catalyst to my father's demise. I needed answers but I did not know where to get them.

One night, about a week after my father's funeral, my mother could not sleep in her bedroom and I was afraid to sleep on my own, so she came to my room and we shared the bed. We still did not have electricity the darkness in the room consumed everything and there was deafening silence that gave me chills; with a loud bang, the glass in the display cabinet came crashing down and glass shattered. My mom and I scrambled up and rushed to the living room trying to turn on the torch. For a moment, we thought that someone had burgled our house. Our tenants also came out of their room with their torches in hand. Knowing what made the loud noise we attended to the display cabinet. The glass shelves had slipped and caused the glasses on it to fall, just one glass was broken; it was my father's favorite glass. I looked at my mother, I trembled and I did not know what to think.

We went back to our rooms after putting everything in 'order'. My mother suggested that we said a prayer. I was still angry with God so I just kept quiet while she prayed; I could not bring myself to say amen. When I opened my eyes, I saw a small blue ball of light that came through the bedroom door, it hovered around the room, and then above us. My mother saw it too; we stared at it in awe and silence. The light hovered for a while and zapped out through the window. We did not talk about it until the morning. The ball of light bothered me; I spent the whole day wondering what it meant or what it was. My mother told her sister-in-law about it and she in turn referred us to an apostolic church healer (the white garment worshippers).

At that time we had sought refuge at a Pentecostal church, some kind of therapy that I felt was unnecessary. I remember there was one Sunday, when I reluctantly went to church, there was going to be a guest preacher from another church; he was said to be one of the best prophets and no problem went unseen in his presence. I remember sitting on the classroom bench, choking in my Sunday clothes. The weather was unbearable and the matchbox classroom was full to the bream. The praise and worship team sang their praise songs while other congregants danced and rejoiced. I remember looking out the window hoping for the service to end. The church's regular Pastor got up to his feet and instructed the choir to sing a worship song, he also instructed all those that were sitting to raise to their feet and 'be immersed' in the song. My mother who was sitting next to me rose in jiffy with the other congregants while I dragged myself up. They sang:

Lion of Judah
We worship you,
Lion of Judah...

I lip synced throughout the song, sulking most of the time. The guest Pastor must have seen my attitude toward the worship song as he got up from his seat and grabbed the microphone from the lead singer and he started to pray. He prayed in tongues, I clasped my hands together and just stared at him. He opened his eyes, I recall him saying, "You should not lose faith in God" and I started contemplating as to why I had gone to church in the first place. I looked at the other congregants, shaking and clapping their hands to the sermon. The blouse I was wearing started to choke the life out of me as the heat in the tiny classroom was increasing. I tried to fix my attention to the drenched Pastor who in short talking spams wiped his mouth with a small white face towel while some sweat escaped from his forehead on to the microphone. He continued to preach with his gaze fixated on the left side of the church where I was seated on.

"My people, I want to tell you that God has a plan!" he shouted and I scoffed, I wondered what type of plan God had for me, not so long ago he took the one thing I loved. His voice boomed across the rectangular shaped room, as he told the congregation how 'good' God was. I recall a woman jumping from her seat and waving her hands in agreement to what the Pastor was saying and the other congregants shouted amen back to her and I started studying her outfit. It was a little too tight for a church service; I was astonished as to how she was able to breathe in a body con dress and worse in the inferno we were in. The Pastor suggested we pray, and ask God to intervene in our lives. I sank in my chair; I came to church that was it; I was not going to pray to HIM. My mother looked at me and nudged me; I tried to ignore her nudging, then the Pastor changed his request.

"*I want everyone sitting in the two rows to my left come to the front,*" and he started to pray in tongues, I thought of course he saw my mom nudging me hence he suggested that. I did not want prayers; I did not want to talk to God.
There I was standing in line with the other congregants, while the Pastor paced up and down the line telling us to raise our hands to the Lord and surrender our all to him. Everyone in the lineup followed the instruction, and I scoffed and halfheartedly raised my hands. The shoes I was wearing were starting to hurt. I remember telling my mother that I did not want to wear them, but they were the only decent shoes I had that were not torn or old. I slipped them off and kicked them to the side. He gave another instruction and the people started murmuring what the Pastor had told us to say. I kept my mouth shut. I was certain that I was not going to tell HIM anything, well except that I was angry with him. He continued to give commands for people to follow and each time I heard shrieks coming from behind me. One peculiar shriek caught my attention, I turned my head and noticed that the woman in the tight dress had 'caught' the spirit and went crashing to the ground. Drama, I thought, I giggled silently. My arms started to hurt; I could not keep them up any longer, so I supported them on the sides of my body. I remember the Pastor

shouting, telling the congregants to keep their hands up, I felt attacked and ambushed. I thought God had teamed up with the Pastor to punish me for not talking to Him. After he was done attending to the woman in the tight dress, he started placing his hands on the people I was standing with, one by one they fell. Maybe it was because of exhaustion but because we were in church, they called it the Holy Spirit's touch.

He came to me; it was my turn to be 'touched' by the Holy Spirit. I wanted to be finished with the whole charade. I wanted to go home and continue to be angry with God. I closed my eyes, started murmuring gibberish. I did not want him to catch me not praying and I had vowed that I was never going to pray. He said to me, "*You are bitter*" and he paused. I opened my eyes and I saw him still standing in front of me. I stared at him, he continued to speak, "*you should forgive yourself, that way God can hear your prayers*" I was stunned, what did he mean by forgiving myself? I was not angry with myself. I did not have any grudges with myself, we blended like cookies and cream, and this Pastor was saying I should forgive myself. I scoffed at his remark. I closed my eyes and let him pray for me, while I debated on why he said I should forgive myself when I wasn't angry at myself but HIM.

I regress.
Now we had another option for 'help', the white garment worshippers. They were going to help me find the 'culprit' behind my father's sudden departure and I was certain of that. The man we were going to see stayed a few kilometers from our home in an area called Ascot. I remember walking from Mtapa with my mother and her sister-in-law; the sun was setting fast, and the breeze was becoming a bit colder. We arrived at the house, a few people where outside waiting in queue. We said our greetings as we stood beside them. The queue moved slower than expected and I started to debate with myself about whether I wanted to know if there was foul play in my father's death. There were two people before our turn came, I stared up the stars had already filled the sky; I saw something shoot across it similar to a shooting star. I thought it was weird as it was too early to see stars shoot across the sky.

We entered the one room apartment; it had a tiny bed and a small side table next to the bed. Across the room next to the entrance was an old crooked wardrobe. My eyes ran up the not so clean walls, and I saw a few if not two posters of what I thought was his favorite singer and a new calendar. He was sitting on his bed clothed in his white church regalia; he seemed like a simple man, a clean-shaven head, and no beard. He was not as scary as I imagined. We sat on the floor as instructed by my mom's sister-in-law while she shared pleasantries with the prophet. I remember feeling uncomfortable and guilty as to why I had resorted to divination. I zoned back in and I heard him ask my mother if she wanted my aunt present during our reading. She offered to leave and wait for us outside; there we were staring at a total stranger who was going to tell us whether my father was murdered or not. He started saying a prayer; I was a bit annoyed considering my relationship with God at that moment. He told us many things, in most cases which did not relate to what we were expecting to hear. He then told us about the tiny blue ball of light that we saw the other day. I was stunned as to how he knew about it before we told him. This made me believe him and everything he was going to say. He told us that it was my father checking in on us, and that he wanted to make sure we were still staying home and were okay.

That gave me some kind of comfort, knowing that my father was still around us. He continued to tell us random things, some I could not relate to, and some that had a little meaning to my life. He spoke to me about the dreams, the visions, and the voices. I did not care about that, My main concern was about my father's death. I agree the dreams and visions took up most of my night and the voices scared the hell out of me, but that did not matter to me at all. The prophet gave us pebbles that we were supposed to put in containers filled with water and bathe with it for some days after the 'ritual' we were to return to him. We never did.

We stopped everything including church, I could not stomach their irrelevant prophesy. They were not telling me what I wanted to hear. I felt like they were more concerned with me joining their sects and following a calling that I did not want to be part of. I did not want to be a prophet; I did not want the gift they saw in me. All I wanted were answers. I was getting tired of the pebbles he was giving us, and the water that was meant for baths, and I felt guilty.

Chapter 3

My family crumbled before me, losing my father was a huge blow that was difficult to get over. Surely, we had extended family, but they felt just that, extended; my uncle was there and helped me get back to school, but it was not the same. It sometimes felt like the relations I knew ended the day my father passed. My new life began; I started school a year after his death, an option I had to choose between moving to South Africa and staying home. I did not want to be separated from my mother; it felt like it was just the two of us against the world. Now we had to adjust to a new way of life; we no longer had the one person who we knew as the breadwinner. We sold some of my father's stuff so that we could clear the electricity bill and get our power back. Most nights I would watch my mother skip meals and give an excuse that she was not hungry, when it was not the case, but we would be running out of food. There were nights when I would cuss at my father for dying; these were nights where I would see my mother struggling to put a smile on my face, trying to give me the same lifestyle we had when my father was alive. I know that in her heart she cursed at him to, but my mother would never showed me her weakness. I tried to call his number once; I think I was still stuck in denial when I did that. I remember the phone call going through, I wanted him to answer, maybe say *hey pumpkin sorry gave you a fright, but I am okay.* I hung up before anyone on the other end answered. I could have been scared, or did not know what I was going to say to him. I dialed the number again, some days after the first trial; it did not go through. I was disappointed, and blamed myself for hanging up the first time. *Maybe if I waited for someone on the other end to answer maybe just maybe...*

I have never known my mother to be a person who opened up when life was taking her for a ride; one of the traits I got from her. Truth be told, I think the only time I saw my mother cry was when my father died and most days after his death. She never complained aloud. I admire her strength. I have always been close with mother some would say too close; it never bothered me, some mistake us for sisters. I got some of my Ndebele traits from her and I should say are one of my best qualities. I have always thought that my mother had the kindest eyes anyone could ever have *of course every child sees their mother that way*; but I had always been able to talk without judgement with her, though my peers depicted her as a strict person; sometimes a little too strict. When she smiles, it feels like all troubles in the world are just mere mosquito bites. She is the best cook I know, taught me most of the stuff I know; not saying I am the world's best cook but thanks to her lessons I know how to make a meal. I recall this one time when my mother prepared lunch for my father and his friends, they could not stop raving about the way she had cooked mopane worms and how tasty they were.

Some even went to the extent of stuffing some in their pockets; I wonder what their wives thought upon seeing oil soaked pockets. Growing up I always knew my mom to be the discipliner and my father the pamperer; like this one time I was in primary school, I must have been in grade two. We had a sports day and I was participating in the sack race tournament, *it was not really a tournament* and I had an empty 50kg sack I was going to use. I do not remember much about the sports day but I remember vividly the events that took place after. One of my friends started to brag about being the best sack racer amongst us. Little miss perfect Lizzy could not say no to a challenge, I tightened the grip on my sack and prepared myself for a win; we had a race on the sidewalks of the shopping centre. We had so much fun that I forgot about the time and did not notice that the sun had set. It must have been around five when I saw my mother, raging like a bull towards me and my friends. It was too late for me to escape, so I just stood there and waited for hell to descend on me. I recall my mother knocking on my shaved head with her knuckle and when I tried to duck, he pulled me up by my ear. One drunk came out of the bar where were standing next to and tried to rescue me from the wrath that was coming. My mother hurled insults at the poor man, who immediately took cover back in the only place that was safe for him_ the bar. She grabbed the sack and my satchel herded me straight home with slaps and scolds. From that time onwards I made sure that I was home the second I knocked off school, I would run making sure that I was not an hour late. Through the spanks and whooping I got from my mother, I received so much love; much more than the beatings.

First day of High School was supposed to be a breeze. Budiriro B College was supposed to be my getaway from the pain I was going through. Continuing with my education was a bittersweet moment for me, I was going to carry on dreaming, but my father was not going to be part of that dream. It was a plan we had together before his passing, considering I was still 'young' according to him. All decked up in my uniform and my satchel in my hand, I stood with the other new students. Giggles filled the air and I just stood in my corner sulking, wishing that the day would move faster. I was assigned to my class with a number of other cool students that looked like they had everything in order. The school was renting rooms at an Islamic church. I took a seat at the back of the class, a rectangular make shift room made from plank boards. Some of my new classmates called it a 'chitangwena' as it resembled a shack. I found it funny but I do not remember expressing my feeling towards the remark. It was placed on one side of the corridor and it was close to the office and on the opposite side was the classroom for the second year classes. I had signed up for the Arts department, which meant I was going to study Literature and History; because I had my fight with God, I replaced Divinity with Geography. The day moved slowly with me reluctantly introducing myself to new people who were going to be my classmates. I knew that I did not have a story that was cool enough to be classified as a cool girl, so being known was not top priority. The one moment that hurt me the most was when the class teacher asked how many students had a single parent for a guardian. I felt like a Band-Aid had been ripped off a wound that was starting to heal.

I became friends with a couple of girls who walked in the same direction as mine going home. Though I had some things in common with these girls I felt like I did not fit in with them. I tried not to be open with them; we talked about movies and at the time, there was a crazy hype for African movies particularly Nigerian movies. We had so much fun mimicking the actors and fooling around. One other thing that made me feel that I did not connect with the other students especially girls was boys. I remember being set on not having any romantic relationship with boys. I did not want distractions from school and I thought I was too boring to have anyone interested in me_ seriously though who would want to date someone who was as broken as I was, moreover one who was going through a 'phase' that was alien to me. The first boy to ask me to be his girlfriend gave me a difficult time and made going to school dreadful. We had settled in at school for some months and had become well acquainted with everyone. I recall being very annoyed by this boy, worse I could not believe my new friends thought we could be a good match. Our uniform had a black skirt for the girls and a light blue shirt with a red and blue tie that matched our red jerseys. Boys wore a black trouser and the same colors for the top. My suitor wore what looked like suit and he had broad shoulders and a tiny frame that carried him. He was one of the intelligent students in class, that was an admirable factor but I never saw him as a boyfriend type.

I remember gripping uncomfortable feeling whenever he was near or around me. You could swear that I hated him, but that was not the case. I made a vow, I was never going to date while in school, and I was not going to let a boy ruin it. The other reason why I did not want to date while I was still in school was the fear of disappointing my parents. The pressure of being the perfect child played a huge part in my growing up, this could have been because I was the only child, I felt obligated to be 'perfect' and to me that meant not having a boyfriend until I have completed my studies. Attracting boys was one thing I could not avoid; I tried, but it was a fruitless effort each time. I tried to look as geeky as I could and as repulsive as I could imagine; wore a knee length skirt, and folded my socks down to my ankles, it was unfortunate that I did not wear glasses I would have aced the look. I kept to myself when my friends were not around and stuck my nose in my history books. I aimed at finishing my two years at school like that. I did not want to do anything that would stress out my mother, part of my mission to ease that burden I stopped carrying lunches to school. I toughened up we barely had enough food at home and for someone who was used to getting pocket money from my father I had to adjust to my new lifestyle.

I cannot say I was bullied while at high school, I was almost a ghost; though I remember there were three senior girls who came to welcome us on our first day. They were the 'cool girls', they had a creepy aura that exuded from them and I did not want them near me. They threw all sorts of compliments at me and I just smiled and shrugged off. I remember having a nightmare that involved these girls one time, one might think that it was caused by the fear of the girls but this was around the time my psychic abilities were starting to pick up. In the dream the three girls came to me and asked me to join their group, it seemed I was the perfect candidate to be the keeper of their weird snake looking like creature. I remember being jolted up from the dream sweating and almost out of

breath. I told the prophet about the dream at one of our visits before we quit and he told me that these girls were part of an evil 'satanic' faction and they wanted me to be part of it.
I did not believe him; I thought it was one of his antics to get us to be part of his church. The girls gradually started to hate me, I do not know why or how as I did not use any of the prayer stones he gave me. It did not bother me I was happy to return to my ghost mode.

The dreams, the voices, and the visions had become worse while at school. They were haunting me at every waking minute. I remember one time in school while I was reading, I was sitting at the back of the class, and some of my classmates had gone to the other open classrooms to read as well serve for a few that chose to stay with me. I heard a woman's voice, asking me to write down everything she was going to tell me. It was as if she wanted me to write a story about her life, how she and her brother died. I recall writing an eerie and disturbing paragraph before forcing myself to stop. I told my mother about this; shocked and terrified like me she advised me to pray and send that voice away. Scared to bits I said my prayer while entering the school premises and it chased the voice away but this was not the end of everything. This was the first time I in point of fact spoke to God whole-heartedly after my break from him. There was no one else I could talk to, and believed that no one would perchance understand what I was going through. I tried playing the conversation between my classmates and I in my head and all I could hear was my classmates telling me how insane I was; that was if they would bother to grace me with an answer. I concluded that the voice I heard could have been that of a spirit that remained lingering on the school premises considering the other uses it served.

I accepted the gift, it was not as if it was going to go away and seemed to be the only option I had considering the stories I heard about people who had turned it down, or rejected it. They had their lives turned upside down, of course, my life had already turned upside down I doubt it was going to get any worse than it already was. My aunt suggested that I get help to avoid the interruption at school; the voices had grown louder and were much clearer, and most times I could see things sometimes while I was awake and most times in my dreams. It would cause terror within me and sometimes leave me in a state of disarray. She took me to a woman she knew who had helped her with an almost similar situation. I recall being reluctant, what I wanted was to get rid of the gift. We walked up to a four roomed house, it looked tiny than the other four roomed houses in the area. An elderly woman welcomed us at the kitchen door and I assumed she was the owner of the house as well as the one we were supposed to meet. I recall my heart pounding for a while, as we furthered into the house we were directed into another room past the kitchen, the bedroom that also served as her workspace; there were different colored garments hanging from a brown-chipped wardrobe. We were given head wraps to put on our heads and instructed to sit on the floor. My eyes were all over the room and my heart never ceased beating, for some reason I was scared. The woman started praying, her Shona was deep, I could not understand a word she was saying, and I would steal glances at my aunt hoping for a translation.

While praying she splashed some water on my face, I gasped as it caught me by surprise. She at last started speaking in what I could decode. She spoke of the gift that I had acquired; she took a 500ml bottle filled with water, she started praying again this time clasping the bottle in her hand and then gave me the bottle to take home with me with instructions that I add it to my water bath and return with update the next day. I recall being confused and disappointed, however I followed the instructions praying that the gift would go away. That night I dreamt of my neighbor's grandson being attacked by crows and I fought them off and saved the little boy, in the dream I was inside the house. I saw a figure standing by my bedside wearing a white apostolic garment and had a white head wrap that had a yellow cross on it. I woke up more confused, the first thing that crossed my mind was that this figure was perhaps an evil person waiting to attack me. We went back to the apostolic faith healer and told her of the dream; she laughed and said I had reacted fast. She told me that the figure I had seen was ostensibly my *'Ngirozi'* as she would put it. This was supposedly the "Angel" that was going to work with me in this journey of my spiritual enlightenment and I was supposed to buy the same items as I saw in the dream. I was distraught; I did not want to be one of them, my life plan was simple I was going to finish school, find a job and look after my mother. Being one of them meant that I would have to attend their churches that were in open spaces and change everything about myself; at least that is what I thought. I recall crying myself to sleep that night, I could not see myself as a *'Mupostori'* I was certain that this was the end of my life. My mother was worried that if I did not follow as instructed it would ruin my future, so she talked me into buying the required items. Money was not a luxury in our household after my father's passing so every penny was used cautiously.

With the cloths in my life, I felt like I was losing myself. I felt like I was drifting further apart from my peers. We started attending the church; apparently, I was supposed to learn the ways of the prophets, the white garment prophets to be precise. The first Sunday I went to the church I remember feeling scared, it was something I was not used to and somehow, I felt bothered. We were sitting, sweat dripping onto the bare ground that looked as though it too was longing for water just as I was longing for a sign. I wanted any sign that showed me that this was not my place. One of the head prophets rose from the elevated ground he was sitting and preached from a few verses. He had a darker tone on his face that matched his beard, it must have been from the treacherous heat that kissed or rather mauled his face on a daily basis. I say this because from the knees to his feet he was light skinned. They all looked like him; one of the head prophets did not stand at all. I noticed that he walked with the aid of a wooded crutch when he was walking to the shrine; I wondered why they had not healed him yet. The shrine, a bare ground that had a white flag hoisted in the eastern side of it, there also was a clay pot that was filled with water and palm leaves lay by the side. This troubled my mind; I wondered why they would put a clay pot at the church if they were against traditional practices. The men sat paralleled to the women but not in close proximity. After they had preached the word, they had us kneeling in a queue facing the east. The *'madzibaba'* gifted with prophesy would splash water on the person they are praying for. I remember when it was my turn to be prayed for, I felt a painful splash of water going onto my face, and he started praying. He told me about the things I already knew, and that I had to accept the process. I did not want to accept any processes; I wanted to be a normal child. He then gave me a pebble and gave me instructions to put in my bath water for three days and return with whatever information that I might have found out during these three days.

Do you know that feeling when you are going through something and it's just you who gets it? It feels like you are in quicksand and with every wiggle you make, further down you go. The more I used the pebble the more I felt that I was doing the wrong thing. I was scared of what was happening to me and I did not want to go to the shrine, I knew it was not me; not that I was too fancy for it, but sitting in the sun and burning was not my style. I told my mother I was done; I could not let myself be draw into a pit that I did not know where it was leading me. She supported me and we both stopped. I hid the cloths I had bought, deep in a suitcase to make sure that I did not have any contact with it. They tried to get me to return to the church, saying that if I refused, I was going to be punished. I remember meditating on the matter, asking for whatever I was going through to stop or at least give me a chance to finish school.
Then the dreams became more persistent, most times, I would be trapped in the nightmares and wake up with aches all over my body. At times, I would have premonitions of things that were to happen. I recall I had a dream of my twin sister, even though I never knew her I felt that I was in her presence. I was being chased in a dark forest, though I do not remember who was chasing me I recall running and tripping over the huge tree roots that were protruding from the ground. Out of nowhere, appeared hands started to come up from the ground trying to grab hold of me. I remember screaming and I could hear my voice choke as the hands dragged me down into the ground; as I was almost halfway into the ground a person who looked like me came to my rescue, grabbing my hand and pulling me out. As she held me close to her and I panted, trying to catch my breath I could feel that she was someone I knew dearly. In another dream, one I remember as if it had just happened, we were sitting and talking about life, almost as if we were catching up. I told her about how much I missed my father and she mentioned how much she envied that I got the chance to live with mom. She came up with a suggestion; as crazy, as it may sound, she asked if we could switch places, just for a short time. I was reluctant of the suggestion and dragged it out for as long as I could.

This was not favored by the new church that was in our life. They made sure that I understood that the dead were not supposed to interact with the living. This somehow made it feel like they wanted me to disown my twin sister and my father's memories, of which I was not ready to let him go. It was a Pentecostal church, another one, they held revivals and prayer sessions that somehow made me feel that they had subdued the gift; for a while I began to think that maybe it was some evil spirit that had taken over me. I was wrong though, I started having more visions and dreams about the church members, and when I told the Apostles, they would shrug off the warnings and ignore me. It troubled me, I started questioning my existence in the church, I wanted help to get rid of the 'gift', I wanted help to understand it, but it did not come while at this church. The Pastor, a man who could have been in his mid-twenties or initial thirties started a youth revival at the church and they insisted that I join them, I wasn't used to spending the whole day at the Apostle's house and there I felt out of place. We were forced to fast and pray for two weeks before the actual revival; the first three days of fasting were rather painful, I suffered from terrible headaches and nausea. When I told the Pastor about my experiences, he just laughed and said that he would pray for me so that it stops. I did not understand his ideology, here I was falling sick from missing meals the whole day, and I could not take it because of the migraines and he dismissed it saying it was the devil trying to stop me.

The Apostle was a woman her face and posture projecting someone in her primary forties, she was big boned and dark in complexion. She seldom smiled, and I was scared of her. There was something about her that I didn't like, something that screamed fake; her sister was also a pastor at the church, she too was big boned and dark in complexion but somewhat younger than her. I could sense a negative aura around them, but shrugged it off thinking that it was because I was afraid of them. What was obvious was their love for money, it was evident in the way they treated their congregants; those with money were given first preference than those without. They had young girls cleaning, cooking and doing laundry for them during the week; I remember one time they tried to make me part of the youth that "resided" at their house. I was exempted because of school, and because I always dodged them and went home after church services; so, I was present when it was time for prayers after school. The first time I realized the segregation in the church was when it was close to the revival. I had a dream, in this dream there was a giant bird sitting on one of the trees at the Apostle's residence; the bird attacked one of the boys who was part of the choir and when it was about to go it grabbed the Apostle and I woke up. The dream worried me so much that I went and informed the male Pastor who laughed in my face and sarcastically called me 'Joseph the dreamer'. I was broken, and thought if I approached the Apostle herself since she was in the dream, she was going to take it seriously. I remember telling her the dream with tears in my eyes and she told me that I worried too much and they were just meaningless dreams. The night of the revival came, and the boy from my dream also came to church; everyone was singing and praying but my heart was pounding, I knew something bad was going to happen. When the Apostle started preaching, silence engulfed the whole place, I heard a loud rustle in the trees just above where she was standing. The boy from my dream started growling from behind me, he sounded like a beast. The Apostle instructed the ushers to get hold of the boy; she prayed for him and claimed that the Holy Spirit had taken over him. I knew that was not it, but I kept it to myself because they already did not believe me. After the dream and incident, I felt neglected by the church, especially the Apostle, it was even worse when my mother fell sick; the trauma of losing a parent came back. Watching her ailing body, laying on the sofa had me shouting at God. I was certain that he hated me, since he brought all these hardships into my life. I asked the male pastor to pray for her, he was the one who seemed to understand me. I remember crying, begging God not to hurt me by taking my mother; she got better but we stopped going to the church. I stopped going because of the Apostles, their love for money made me doubt that they were genuine envois of God and besides I was moving to South Africa.

My life was changing again. I could not refuse this change, I agreed to it because I could not expect my uncle to take me to Varsity after A' level. I had accepted that I was no longer in a position to be making demands or requests, a simple yes, sufficed. I was slowly slipping into depression, everything seemed to be happening fast, and I felt as if I was being forced into a life that was not meant to be mine. Nights towards the day I was going to leave, saw me crying and thinking about what would happen to my mother if I left. It was going to be the first time; I was going to away from my mother.

Chapter 4

There I was, feeling cold and mesmerized by the lights that filled the night sky. I remember trying to hide my puffy eyes from my uncle, and all I wanted was to go back to my mother. Being in a new country frightened me. I did not know what to expect, of course, I was going to live with family, but I was not used to being miles away from everything I knew. South Africa was not the same as Zimbabwe, I had heard that everything moved fast, and the lights were brighter, and the nights were darker. Now I was in the same place they told me was God forsaken. I felt like every person I met, knew that I was a stranger. I felt lost.

I moved to South Africa at nineteen, still innocent, and naïve, and the bubble I grew up in was instantly popped. I had managed to subdue the gift, I did not want to scare off the people I was going to be staying with; heck, it scared the crap out of me, I dare not mention how my mother reacted toward it. I, with great difficulty ignored the voices and the dreams and somehow, they became blocked. Strangely, from nowhere I had picked up a peanut allergy; the so-called prophets linked it with the 'gift', and I did not understand how that moved hand in hand.

Prior to my arrival in the foreign land, everything seemed to be following a perfectly laid out plan. I was going to continue with my education; University was in the plan, and then find myself a good paying job and take care of my mother, just as I promised my father I would. I welcomed the idea of me continuing with school, I figured I was still young and school was the only reasonable option. Then I remembered my mother, she had just lost her husband and probably had nothing planned for a life without him. When my uncle came with the 'idea' of me working 'part-time' I thought it was good plan, as I could be able to work, help my mother and study at the same time. I felt that my stars were aligning.

A few days after my arrival, my uncle asked me to go with him to a meeting in Pretoria. It must have been his way to make me feel welcomed. We met his clients at a restaurant, which I do not quite remember the name; the waiter came to us and gave us menus. I did not want to seem too forward so I just sat in my chair quietly going through the menu. They discussed what they had met for while I struggled to understand why the restaurant sold monkey gland sauce. Seeing this confirmed all that I had heard of South Africa, and they were even worse, they made sauces out of monkey glands. MONKEY GLANDS. I wondered what else they made from wild animal parts. I wondered about the food that I was going to order since everything was foreign to me. As the meeting ended, my uncle and his business friend summoned for the waiter who came with a huge smile plastered on his face. He asked what we wanted to eat; I glanced back at the menu as if I had no looked at it before. My choices were between a burger drenched in monkey gland sauce, prawns and ribs with chips and other fancy food with weird sauces, I had no idea what they were. I was never not going to choose the one with the monkey sauce it already disgusted me without even seeing it. I looked at my uncle for help he must have noticed my plight, so he ordered a salad for himself and the ribs with prawns for me. The food came and so did the trouble of eating it; I stared at what they called prawns. They were creepy pink creatures staring back at me. I did not know how to eat them; it was my first time seeing these creatures let alone eating them. I evaded them as long as I could, by eating the ribs and the chips until my uncle noticed it. He took one prawn from my plate, and I eyed him as he shelled them and removed the head until white flesh was left. I copied his technique and within minutes, I became a pro at eating prawns. And I should say they tasted way better than they looked, I guess it is true what they say *don't knock it 'till you try it.*

Finding a job was somewhat easy; my uncle was connected, knew exactly, where I had to start looking, and within a month, I found myself in an upscale mall in Johannesburg North called Montecasino, as a runner at the Gourmet Garage, wiping tables, and scraping vomit off bathroom floors. He used to work there, and he remained linked to the place well after he left.

I was awe struck the first time I entered Montecasino, the security at the entrance had metal detectors that they used to search for guns and other weapons. Everyone looked merry pacing up and down, in and out the many shops that where in the mall. I could hear jovial screams and shrieks coming from the casino side, my uncle told me that people were celebrating their winnings from the slot machine. He warned me to stay away from the casino; apparently, many people had lost their life savings to the machines and tables. I was still dumbfounded by the awesomeness of the mall to be interested in the casino. He took me to the restaurant I was going to work at; as if strategically placed in a corner, it was not hard to miss. The green and grey tablecloths, though bright and loud, seemed to be out shined by a red beetle (you know the ones with the boot in the front and engine at the back) that was parked by the entrance. And I, was as a cat drenched in water, hiding behind my uncle as he conversed with the restaurant manager who was more than happy to have me join the team, or family as she said.

I remember my first night as a waiter's assistant, they called us runners; I was frightened, and had my eyes popped out, gawking at everything that was in sight. The waiters were friendly and helped me out with my training and I remember trying not step on any of my new bosses' toes. Especially Mr Black, he scared me; it must have been is deep English accent or his dilated pupils whenever he gave out orders. He had pixie black hair that had a few strands brushing his forehead and the sides trimmed off. His fair skin resembled that of an American actor. He was about an inch taller than I was, and was definitely easy on the eyes even when he was fuming with rage; still I was terrified of him and Mr Nick

who never spoke casually but scolded me for resting my foot on the wall when I was tired. I was ready to quit by knock off time, which by the look of things was far.
I had never been in an environment where I was surrounded by that many white people. I remember the first night, spending it in hidden, dark corners trying to avoid white people and any other person who seemed to have interests in talking to me. I was very much confident with speaking in English; I did not fear that, however, I was scared to be close to them, not because I was scared of white people even though they were double if not more than the number of whites I had been around. I hated how they fussed over me and made me the center of attention, as if I was not of this world. It was like school all over again being a new comer.

I eventually got used to the new faces I saw every day. I started to enjoy conversing with new people, I even discovered food, different types of it, and how it was prepared. Something I had limited knowledge of serve that I got from the TV cooking shows. I came across my arch nemesis, monkey gland sauce and I thought to myself while reading the menu, why South Africans loved eating monkeys, did they perhaps adapt to the norms of Congolese? I asked one waiter, I had grown acquainted with *why do you serve monkey gland sauce? Does it taste good?* The waiter looked at me; he must have picked up my concern of killing monkeys and making sauce out of their glands. *You should try it;* I remember him saying with so much conviction that I was considering to do so. *It's great with meat and on burgers.* He continued to say, even though I had already worn a disgusted look on my face. *Is it really monkey gland?* He chuckled, *no dear, it is an onion chutney*; I did not believe him, so why call it monkey gland instead of onion chutney or simply onions in brown sweet sauce, I thought. Then I tried it, after hours of show and tell from the kitchen staff just to ease my conscience. It was not that bad.
Most times, (when I was not worried about the menu items), being in the restaurant business was painful, (especially the first days); I would be questioned as to why I was working at a young age. I call it the vampire's curse, looking younger than my age was something I inherited not sure from which side of my family_ but it had tongues wagging. Some even offered to call the police or anyone who dealt with child labour to 'save' me. I did not know how to explain to them that I had to be here working, earning, and creating a new life for myself, possibly the plight of every Zimbabwean that was done with High school and was one parent short.

Running after grown men and women wiping their spills and vomit was not something, I had seen myself doing after school; but I was here, doing it. And slowly, I started hating my life. It was the type of hate that came with disappointment and a strong stench of failure. I felt as if I was being punished for something and like a slave than an employee. I used to cry as I cleaned the mirrors in the toilets. My reflection was that of a lost cause. I cried because a part of me knew that this life was not the life my father had seen for me, when we daydreamed under the mango tree.
I remember being afraid of getting lost; and it would have taken a split second for me to be lost in the massive Montecasino mall. I would mark my location with a landmark and move accordingly keeping it in sight, every time I had to go on my lunch break. The first thing I marked my location with was the steel bench that was just outside the entrance of

the restaurant, I would walk around the huge mall keeping the bench insight. The second thing I marked with was the red beetle that was parked outside the restaurant. Montecasino was an Italian themed mall with a brick pavement and washing lines with clothes running across the roof. There were streetlights along the pathways and street signs with directions; it gave the feel of a real street of a town. During the day, the roof resembled the blue skies with a few wispy clouds and in the night, a blanket of stars covered the ceiling. At times, it was difficult to tell what time it was as they would alternate the stars and blue sky just to be met by a blinding light when you went outside. The lawns outside were a lush green and well maintained by the grounds man who paid meticulous attention to it. The place bustled with people moving in and out of the numerous restaurants. It was pointless going to lunch though, especial the first few days, I only had enough money for transport as it doubled in price at night when we knocked off. I would walk around the mall, window shopping and eyeing the bench or the car depending on which direction I had taken in the first place. I would walk past other restaurants and see families, complete families having a meal or ice creams, and I would wish if my father were here and my mother and we too would be sitting next to the fountain stuffing our faces with spaghetti _my favorite. After an hour's walk, I would go back to the restaurant with my stomach growling *nothing a glass of water wouldn't muffle*, then I would grab my dry cloth and pin it on my side and stuff a wet cloth in a tiny plastic bag into my back pocket. I would move around, checking tables and doing anything to keep my mind from thinking about food. *Imagine fighting off the smells coming from the kitchen.* I would only have to wait ten more hours 'till I knocked off and hopefully find something to eat if not that meant I was going to eat the next day.

Working in restaurants exposed me to a world that was very different from the one I knew. I was a 'protected child', exposed only to the things that maybe were important at that moment and throughout school because of this, I tried with much failure to fit in with others. I found myself faced in that situation in South Africa. I was in this huge classroom with students who came from all backgrounds and had experienced all forms of life. I felt lost and being in my uncle's home made me feel more of a stranger than family. I felt unwanted, as if I had suddenly become a burden to them even though I was working. The feeling became worse when I came home to empty plates.

I was paying my way through school, but still I felt like I was not living up to my uncle's expectations. As if, I was not making him proud enough. This made me miserable, and depressed; all my efforts seemed to go unnoticed and I was slowly fading, becoming a ghost. Maybe I was having trouble with adjusting to my new surroundings some would say. I would keep my mind busy so that I would not overthink about the situation that I had found myself in; I took up double shifts at the restaurant to try to tire out my body and mind. When I was not working, I escaped the prison I had found myself in by submerging myself in cold water. I would sink myself in the complex swimming pool, and listen to the muffled shouts and giggles of my cousin playing with her friends.

I did not know how to swim, still do not, but I knew how to drown. Drowning myself, was the only way I knew how to deal with the pain that I harbored as well as the stresses that were lurking; waiting for me to crack. They drowned, the memories of my father, the

lingering pain, feeling inadequate, and unwanted. The water embraced me; the cool cuddles soothed the wounds. They all drowned when I sank into the water and came up with me when I surfaced.
This was my first year I was in South Africa and I was a puppy taken from its mother, all I did was yelp silently at night and wear a smile on my face in daytime. Everything felt forced on me, as the pressure piled up on me and all I could do was bottle it up.

I was stabbed, accidentally while I was at work.
Initially, I did not feel the knives pierce my skin; yes knives, I thought I had just bumped into a waiter who was rushing to get his table of eight set. I never thought that I had been stabbed.
Absent-minded, I made my way to my post, the door_ I became a host for the restaurant a few months of being a waiter's assistant, but alternated into the latter when the restaurant was busy, Mr Jay, the other manager, noticed blood seeping through my white shirt and alerted me of the red stain. I glanced at my chest area and the stain was just under my left breast with a gentle press on it, I felt a sharp pain reciprocating the touch and more blood oozed out. I started to ponder about how I could have gotten hurt. The poor waiter who had stabbed me rushed to me as I went upstairs to the bathroom to nurse my wound and clean my shirt, he told me about the little accident that had befell me at his expense.

He told me what had happened and I was stunned.
I had no idea that I had had such a close encounter with death and I did not notice it. He apologized and I remained dumbfounded for the rest of the night. I had not realized that stress had taken over my life to that extent.
Mlungisi had become an older brother in the short time I had been working there and I was certain that he would never hurt me on purpose. He nicknamed me *Njunju*, he said it meant beautiful girl in Kasi talk. He would help me carry the huge crate that contained sauces down the stairs and occasionally buy me lunch. He was an average height person and his dark complexion shimmered under the restaurant lights. He did not speak much when he was sober but after a few smokes he presented a jovial mood that lifted the whole restaurant's mood and sometimes annoy the bosses. Most times, I would see him standing in the quiet corners of the restaurant and wonder what went through his head. Maybe he was like me, yearning to go back home or maybe he wanted that place he would fit in; I never asked him what he thought about during those quiet moments, but I could tell that the stabbing incident really shook him, probably at the same level it surprised me.

Chapter 5

I had moments that made my life somewhat fun. I should say these little good moments made me feel human, just like my second crush.
I was on my morning shift as waiter's assistant before my evening shift as the host when I met him; I had finished my duty of filling up the sauce bottles early so I decided to do my plate collection run at the City Lodge Hotel. I walked slowly, thinking about my situation and meditating on the thought of going home for Christmas even though it was a few months away. I heard a male voice calling out to me offering to help me with the crate I was carrying. I turned to see a car with four men in it, they all seemed hyped up, and I was terrified of them thinking they were some of the criminals I had heard of. I forced a smile at the man who was sitting in the back seat without paying much attention to him and told him I was okay with the crate in the friendliest manner I could have said it. I picked up my pace, making sure I was close to the security of the Hotel, as I entered the Hotel premises the car pulled up behind me. Promptly, thoughts that they were after me filled my head, I did not think that they could possibly be heading to the same place as I was. I arrived at the reception and chatted briefly with the girls that were at reception and they told me about the other plates that were still in the hallway of the third floor. Feeling a bit lazy, I decided to take the elevator and, the men from the car also went in the same elevator as the one I was in.

Then 'he' started a conversation and I, keeping my face fixed to the ground made sure my answers were short and precise. What I picked up from his voice was that he had an accent and it was quite flattering. It was my first time interacting with a person who had what I thought at the time was a French accent. He asked me if I worked in the hotel and I responded. Told him about the restaurant that had the best burgers in town; Gourmet Garage. He told his friends that he wanted to try the restaurant out, and his friends started to speak in a language that I was hearing for the first time since I had been staying in South Africa. It was not any of the South African languages, I remember lifting my head and looking at them, and I saw him stealing glances at me but I quickly diverted my eyes to the elevator door avoiding eye contact.

When I reached the third floor, I said my goodbyes to them and carried on with my work. On my way back to the restaurant, the thought of the men in the elevator had totally slipped my mind and upon my arrival, I was received with an order that needed to be delivered at the hotel by lunchtime. I hated such orders as it required me to keep checking on the time and being a perfectionist had caused me a lot of anxiety. When it was lunchtime, I took the order; on my way I would play a guessing game, I would try to

guess type of guest I was delivering food to and the amount of tip he or she might give me. The delivery was on the fourth floor, the last room in the hallway; I thought it might be a woman, I had been delivering to women from earlier that day. That and the size of burger the person ordered, men usually ordered double burgers or extra chips; this order was just a simple burger with pepper sauce. I came up to the room and knocked on the door, and shouted *delivery!* A familiar accent said shouted back *"okay, one moment."* The door opened, and I was received by a shirtless dark chocolate toned man, whose face was quite familiar. His abs, fully built I thought that it was probably because he went to the gym. He smiled,
"See, I told you that we were fated to meet." I casted my eyes slightly to the side, as I tried to signal to him that he was half-naked.
"It's just a coincidence," I told him, with my eyes still shifted away from him.
"Coincidence? No!" He chuckled and invited me into his room with his meal. I tried to decline his invite but he walked away before I could speak. *"You can drop that anywhere you can, lemmie get my wallet."* He instructed as he paced up and down the room, flipping sheets, pillows and some of his clothes that were on the bed. He looked comfortable, in his semi-nude state than I was while looking at him fumbling for his wallet under the sheets and under bed. *"I'm sorry, I thought I had my wallet somewhere here,"* he flipped the sheets and the pillow as I placed his meal on a small table next to the T.V. I cleared my throat as I repositioned the tray that was clutched under my arm and glanced at the swipe machine that was in my hand. I then moved towards the door with my back turned against it, I then stood by the doorway, *just in case he tried something sneaky.* After some uncomfortable moments standing by the doorway, he found it and paid for his meal, I thanked him and turned as quickly as possible making my way for the hallway, as I was about to leave, he stopped me. *"I didn't catch your name,"* he smiled and a dimple formed on his right cheek. *"Elizabeth, I'm sorry I thought I introduced myself before"* He rested his hand on the side of the door, leaning the right side of his body on it and exposing his chiseled torso. "*I'm Neo, are you South African*?" I shifted my eyesight to his face with much difficulty, I smiled back, blushing a little and tried to hide it and keep myself as composed as I possibly could. His eyes glimmered when he smiled, the looked like black pearls shining under the moonlight.
"*I'm not South African, I'm Zimbabwean."* Wrinkles formed on his forehead and he cleared his throat.
"*You don't sound Zimbabwean though,*" he smiled. I was used to people telling me that. I checked the time on the swipe machine, he noticed the way I might have been worried about the delay, "*Why don't you give me your number*?" I felt reluctant to give away my number, but I gave him anyway and he gave me his number. I left the floor and the hotel; I had spent thirty minutes on the delivery; not that I was counting but it was one of the longest trips I had taken and I was a bit worried that I was going to be in trouble with my bosses. He was my first real friend outside work.

Later that day he called me after my shift, and invited me to his room to chill and watch movies. I declined, it was around midnight, and I was exhausted; besides, to me, he was still a stranger due to my upbringing I could not easily hang out with strange men that too at night. When I refused his invite, he came to my work place and he found me sitting on one of the stone benches outside the mall waiting for my ride home. My driver was becoming a regular latecomer and this day was one of those days. Neo sat with me and we talked, well he did most of the talking while I stared at him, admiring his accent. I was lost in his tales of Angola his home country and his journey to South Africa. He was coy, kept making jokes; I guess he hoped they would make me feel comfortable around him and it did work a little; I was not as up tight as earlier in the day. We spoke and for that short time, I liked talking to him, it helped me forget the stresses I had for a while, and I felt wanted and loved.

My friendship with my Angolan Angel grew; it felt like he did not want anything in return and that eased my soul whenever I met up with him. He would wait with me every night while I waited for my ride and we would spend the few hours talking about movies and music, sometimes he would tell me about his dreams and what he wanted from life. He returned to his home country, after his contract was over; his absence was quite visible, I would not wait for my regular ride because waiting became boring. We continued to chat over the phone, even during my shifts I would sneak into the bathroom and reply to his texts.

Chapter 6

I then met him, my would-be knight in shining amour. I was sitting in one of the hallway booths of Molly's bar. My new driver worked there as a bouncer, so waiting for him to knock off was the only option I had for me to get home, even if it meant I had to wait for hours. He walked in with his friends and they seemed to be drunk, they shouted at the top of their voices, all except him. His friends walked past me but he stopped,
"hello there," he threw himself in the chair across me. I looked at him brow furrowed I was annoyed of the beer stench that exuded from him, and simply because he was total stranger.
"Hello." I kept my focus on my phone and tried to plug the other earphone into my ear, hoping it would annoy him and make him leave.
"I'm Dan," he introduced himself and asked for my name. *"Elizabeth,"* I kept my answer short hoping it will make the conversation shorter and chase him away. I made the mistake of smiling because it made him more comfortable and he leaned forward with his elbows planted into the table. "*Can I get you another orange or is it mango juice*?" He pointed at my half-full glass of orange juice that my driver had given me. I refused his offer bearing in mind that he was a total drunk stranger.
"*No thank you, I'm okay with the one I have,"* I smiled again. I have no idea why I kept smiling at him when I actually wanted him to leave me alone. He talked for a while before his friends started to call out to him; I kept my answers short and uninteresting as I possibly could. He quickly gave me his business card, and I was stunned to discover that he was an architect. The way he appeared did not do any justice to his occupation. He noticed how I quickly slipped the business card in my purse and took out his phone nagged me to give him my number. He must have thought that I was going to throw the card away. I did, hoping that because he was drunk he might forget to save it or lose it immediately.

Around midnight or could have been a few hours after, the bar closed and my new friend left at the same time as I did. I remember him asking me if I was going to be safe as I got in my ride home. I was surprised that a stranger cared enough to ask about my safety. While in the car, I received numerous texts from him checking if I had arrived home. When I got home, he continued texting me until I fell asleep. As days went by, our chats became regular; his work kept him busy most of the time and so did mine. His drinking partners rarely made their way to the restaurant that I worked at and if they did come, I would be off duty and pretty much too tired or too stressed out to hang out, moreover going out was not something I enjoyed doing. My friendship with Dan was different from Neo's; he was more of a suitor than a friend. I cleverly evaded the pursuits by telling him that I was busy all the time and simply ignoring the topic whenever he started it.

I was scared to start dating, do not know why but I felt that I was not ready to do that, besides work kept me occupied. In fact, I am certain that no part of my brain thought about dating, it was a topic never discussed in my head. Surely, I had crushes here and there, but I never let them grow beyond that. Sometimes I think that I never dated or thought about dating because I did not want to do something that would make my uncle disappointed in me. I was at a point in my life where I was extremely cautious with everything, I was doing just so I do not become a disappointment. It felt as if I was under a microscope, especially with my uncles; so, I became a 'nun', friend zoned every man that I met, but I could only keep this 'sister act' for a certain period. I gave excuses, took advantage of the late hours and early starts at work and besides I barely had time to socialize outside of work. I was too bothered to be fraternizing with anyone; I had dreams that haunted me at night that is if I managed to sleep. My loud thoughts took up most of my mind wondering what my life had turned into; mostly I think it was because I missed my mother, I missed being home, and being in South Africa made me feel like I did not know who I was. For months, I evaded Dan's pursuits and maintained our friendship.

I never liked the route I took to reach my driver, but I had no choice. It was either I walk there, or be stuck at the restaurant, it might have seemed safer with the Montecasino security there, but they did not want any staff standing around outside for long hours, as it would seem suspicious. *They always suspected the waiters and cleaning crew of some devious act,* maybe it was because we were black or because we were foreigners. They once saw me sitting on the concrete bench by the fountain, waiting for my transport home. The Montecasino security came in their white bakkie; they flashed their torch at me. I shielded my eyes and they dimmed the light, asked me if I was okay, and needed any help. I responded telling them that I was waiting for my ride home. They flashed the torch in my face again; I think they wanted to get a better look. The one security man in the driver's side said something through his radio and tapped his partner on the shoulder and they drove off. They would return after a few minutes and stall then drive off. It made me feel rather uncomfortable, as if I had committed some crime by sitting there. A new law came in, outside cars were not to be seen on the premise; by outside cars they meant the cars that pick up the mall staff. That meant I had to walk, down a paved pathway with streetlights shining my way, then through a dark hundred-meter passage with giant tree branches hovering above like creepy fingers reaching out to grab me. After crossing the main road that was dead quiet by that time, I would find my way inside the fence of a shopping mall. Here my heart paces slowly while my feet quickens theirs, this part of my route wasn't too scary, the lights were brighter and there were a few clubs that would be bustling with people. Clutching my bag tightly to my chest, I would make my way to the back of the Spar; a grocery shop, and I then slither through a tiny gate that faced another road, dark and gloomy. I could hear my feet tapping on the tarred road as I scampered through the dark hundred-meter walk to reach the gate leading to the mall where Molly's Bar was located. Then exhale.

Chapter 7

Making friends in South Africa was easy however; it did not make me feel at home. I was around people on a daily basis but felt lonely and miserable. My happy moments only lasted as long as the days in winter, the only time they were long was when I came back home; like when I was informed about a wedding that was taking place back home. Time away from work during the December holidays was all I wanted. I had already started saving up some money, planned to buy my mom a dress that she would wear to the wedding. There was great feeling that came with being able to provide stuff she wanted or needed. It made me feel grown up; I felt I had become a responsible human being. I was a few responsibilities away to fulfilling the promise I made to my father.

December 2015, I recall the lengthy conversation I had with my mother one night, this was the first night in Zimbabwe; I explained everything to her in detail, all the things I told her over the phone calls. I could tell that all the things I was telling her were breaking her from within. A deathly silence engulfed the room as she looked at me with worry written all over her face. I could see that she wanted to help me; she did not know how to do that. I knew how she felt because I did not know how to help myself either, but confiding in her felt like the first step that I needed.

Trembling hands, cranky mood, and a glum look almost resembling that of an alcoholic who has not gotten her fix yet, graced my face that morning. She noticed that something was wrong with me.

I told her it was because of work, I got hooked on coffee, of course she believed me, the long hours I clocked in daily was enough evidence. Truth is, the coffee kept my mind up, keeping me away from the constant bickering of the voices in my head and torture that ate me up. Coffee held my tears back; it stopped me from feeling sad, it muffled the melancholic memories that swam nonstop in my head. It made me happy; those few minutes that I spent high on caffeine, were my happiest. Coffee became my true love and only true friend. I became somewhat of a coffee connoisseur; I could tell freshly ground exported coffee from the coffee that had been shelved for far too long. My tongue had become acquainted to the various tastes the caffeinated beverage had to offer. I would trail the steam from my cup and indulge on the smell as it lingered on the tiny hairs in my nostrils, with a deep breath I could feel it making its way to my heart and gently caress the wounds. Sometimes when I could not get any hot water, I would lick the dry granules from my palm, and close my eyes as the bitter taste tickle my taste buds and then I would carry on with my day. This was normal to me, and I was certain that it was safer than alcohol.

Few days after my arrival, we had a wedding to attend. Another family gathering filled with more fake smiles, giggles, and laughter. Then how are you? And I have missed you; everyone pretending to be nice to each other.
My aunt *the bride* saw me fuddle two cups of coffee one morning while everyone was dashing about sorting wedding stuff. Coffee kept me distracted while I was at my uncle's place.
"Lizzie I saw you drinking coffee earlier on, are you having another one?" She questioned while turning the kettle to help the other women to make breakfast.
"Have you eaten anything yet?" I was still collecting myself to answer the first questions as she threw another one in my face.
"It is the only way I can get functional," I responded pulling a tub of margarine and loaves of bread to start buttering.
"You started this in S.A right?" she asked, pouring the boiled water into a pot that was place on the stove.
"Yeah." I took a sip of what had now been my third cup. I saw the disapproval on her face, her doctor instincts had kicked in. I was about to get a lecture on caffeine and how bad it was for me in high amounts. I could feel it.
"You should cut down, try something else..." one of my cousins flew in the kitchen interrupting the talk. Technically, she saved me. *Thanks, cuz.*
I was home, the only place where I was supposed to be me. That meant forgetting my depression. I was in no space to start talking about my troubles. I had already done it with my mom.

Most if not all of the people that were at the venue were perfect strangers, I had not talked to them ages. Everyone acted as of each of them lived in each other's backyard. Smiles plastered on everyone's faces and laughter choking any other sound that might have been there. They all seemed happy to see each other, and that fakeness stifled me. I found myself slithering out of the crowd and looking for a quiet space. Somewhere, where I could not dampen anyone's mood.
"Why don't you try writing?" a friendly voice echoed behind me during one of my moments; sitting in silence watching the orange sky complimenting the setting sun. I turned my head and saw a tall figure, light in complexion with a friendly smile standing behind me with a glass of orange juice in hand. He came and sat on a concrete bench beside me and said hello.
"Hie." At first I felt uncomfortable talking to him, I wanted him to leave quickly before my mother or my uncle saw me. *"You are from the groom's side, right?"* He said making himself comfortable.
"Yes, he is my uncle." I kept my answer short, hoping that he would leave me alone. *"How come I didn't see you on the bridal team?"* I took a sip of my evening cup of coffee. I always had one or two to help me sleep. *"I don't dance. Are you on the bridal team?"* I asked avoiding a why do not you dance question. He told me that he was one of the groomsmen and he was related to the bride. Knowing that we were almost family gave me some sort

of comfort; I knew what I was going to tell my mom or uncles if they found me sitting with him. The last thing I wanted was my uncles pestering me about boyfriends, when I did not intend to have one at that time.

He asked me why I was drinking coffee on a ridiculously hot day, I remember telling him that it cooled me down; which was a lie obviously, I never opened up to people. I had mastered the art of seeing where any conversation was going and quickly make it about them if they tried to steer it and ask questions about me.
"You said something about writing, do you write?" He smiled, he introduced me to a type of writing that took the tone of poetry but the form of prose he said they were Pisces. He told me that it helped him scare away the ghosts that haunted him. I did not bother to ask what ghosts they were; I had my own, and coffee kept them at bay. Something about the way he spoke about writing that was drawing, as if it was celestial. He had a smile on his face that spewed satisfaction, as if he had won all the battles life had thrown at him.
"Lizzie please bring me some water in my room," my aunt summoned me to her bedroom the wedding was over and the family was sitting in the living room sharing the day's events. I took a bottle of water and a glass, and knocked on her door.
"Come in!" she shouted but calmly. I went inside and found my uncle leaning against the dressing table; my aunt applying cream on her hands, sitting on the bed in her white silk gown.
"How are you doing dear, we didn't have much time to talk because of the wedding." I smiled and responded. I handed her the water she had asked for. Then she asked me about South Africa, if I had adjusted well enough and if school was going well among other things. We had a long chat, part of it felt as if they were trying to get some information out of me, or maybe it was just me being my paranoid self. I had slowly started to stop trusting people; it must have been my defense technique. I do not know it just happened.
"Don't you want to come to Australia?" She asked. I wanted to scream yes, I thought maybe if I ran away from Africa maybe I will find my place on another continent. Maybe Australia was going to be my escape.
As I was thinking of an answer, I remembered that my uncle had given me a chance after my father's death. *"I'm still studying that side, if the offer still stands I will come for a visit or after my course is done."* I felt somewhat indebted to him, and thought maybe if I forced myself one more time I would find a way to make him proud. I did not know if I wanted to go to Australia, I was not sure if I was ready for it. I was certain about where I stood when it involved me going back to South Africa. I did not want to go back there, but I had no choice.
I kept contact with Tinashe, *the boy from the wedding*. After the wedding we exchanged numbers and from that time he would send me his writings; pushing me to also write. I never considered taking it seriously. I was not in the right space of mind to write poetry, even though I kept I diary, one I wrote down my pain. At first I felt as though writing poetry made me feel worse, I found it useless, especially when he died. I lost all hope, it was as if he was writing his way to death and the ghosts won, was I ever going to win my battle? He was the only person that understood me even when I shared nothing about the

things I was struggling with. I felt like I was being punished, as if I was destined to never fit in the world and everything that I cherished was meant to be taken away from me, first my father and then this guy that showed me a way to face my demons. For a while, I thought he was the escape I was waiting for.

I then quit coffee, it was not easy, but I had to do it. Coffee no longer silenced the voices, they got used to the chicory taste. They seemed to speak louder and mock me even more. Maybe the coffee home was not strong enough. Maybe something in the water tamed it and became my kryptonite.

Chapter 8

Leaving home again was painful, it resurrected feelings of being robbed and forced into a life that I really did not want. I regretted declining the offer to go to Australia and I regretted not being able to say no, to returning to South Africa. I felt trapped.
The only reason that made me to go back there, was the proud look on my mother's face when I could do stuff for her, like covering the cost and paying for whatever she might have wanted. Moreover, I had school; I had enrolled myself at a college, trying to continue with the real plan 'we' had when I initially left for South Africa. The plan that fell through, changed suddenly, and ruined my trust for people. The only reason I took up Human resource management was to impress my uncle, I wanted to hear him say he was proud of me. It was something that was missing in my life; those few words when a father smiled and said he was proud of their child.

There were times my taxi drivers would play the role of shrinks, unknowingly they would boost my spirit and give me advice on things that I would never dare to share with them. They would say things that would open up my eyes to a world that I was closed off, like this one driver a Nigerian national. I never knew his name because I was so scared of him to the point of not asking or conversing with him. I always had a stereotypical image of Nigerians mostly encouraged by the Nigerian movies; according to the films, they were loud, and associated with a whole lot of criminal activities as well as known voodooists. I tried to maintain my emotional distance with my driver. He however proved me wrong; he was an amazing person, from the position of his car seat he seemed like a tall man. He had a dark skin tone and a well-chiseled face with strong masculine features. His baldhead was always shiny, I wondered if he polished it every night, he came to pick us up. His cologne gave me a hard time but he always made sure my ride home was comfortable always, except for this one time. It was not entirely his fault but was one of the worst rides home that I had ever experienced.

I had called him just after midnight, on a Friday one of the busiest nights at the restaurant that saw us knocking off late. He came to pick me up at my work place; we drove a few metres to another restaurant where he picked up three more girls. After he checked the time, I guess he realized that he was way past his knock off time. He suggested that we drive past the bus stop where almost half the staff hitchhiked to get home.
When we arrived there, the driver slowed down he murmured something that sounded like *"those men are here too,"* I tried looking around to see if I could see what he saw. I could not see anything then suddenly he started speeding up. I looked at the dashboard

and saw that the speedometer and saw that he had passed the 160km/hr. mark. It was an unusual thing for him to drive past the speed limit; I looked through the rear view mirror and noticed a car speeding up to my side of the car. Suddenly a loud bang clanged on my side, my heart jumped; scared I looked over my left shoulder and saw a big bald man smashing the left side of the car with a huge stick with a thick knob. He looked like he was rabid, except there was no foam at the mouth as an infected dog would act; insults rolled off his tongue fiercely. The men in the car were shouting at the driver to pull over and he ignored their efforts. They drove over to the driver's side and hit his side with what looked like knobkerrie.

I remember clinging onto the girl, I was sharing the seat with, and the driver leaned over the steering, extended his hand to the floor, and reached for something under his seat. He kept his left hand on the steering and his eyes on the road. The men after us did not stop hitting the sides of the car and they hurled insults at our driver in the process. My heart was pounding, and then it stopped when I saw him pull out a gun from under his seat. I started thinking of all of the nights I rode in his car, wondering if the gun was always there. He must have done something to the gun as it made a sound that sent terror to every inch of my body. He looked like someone who was ready to shoot at the men chasing us if they happen to shoot at us first. I said silent prayers, hoping that a shoot-out would not happen with us in the car. The banging and the shouting made all of us in the car scared to death; he doubled the speed of the car while swerving to distract the car in pursuit. The car that was in pursuit slammed itself on the driver side; there was a loud bang and the car swerved almost out of the road, the driver avoided what could have been an accident with his gun still in hand. I closed my eyes and continued to pray even harder, under my breath. The people sitting in the back seat screamed, the driver noticed the distress that was in the car and he made a turn and I saw him entering a police station.

He parked in front of the door of the station and yelled for the police to come and help us. He told them about the whole ordeal and the station commander ordered two officers to check. He handed the girl I was sitting with the gun; she could not hide it in her purse so she passed it on to me because I had a bigger bag. I remember pressing the bag against my chest and felt my heart pounding even harder. One police officer ordered a search; I think this was after they heard the driver's accent, which was always a red flag raiser amongst law officials. I was shaking like a leaf on a windy day, I thought they were going to find the gun in my bag and I would be arrested. My bowels were turning against me; it was as if I had ingested a handful of laxatives. I thought of explanations that were going to save me from jail time. The search was called off after they discovered that we were all waiters. The Nigerian driver asked the police to give us an escort at least until he delivered everyone home. We got in the car, the police instructed the driver to drive out, and they would follow behind us. When our car was back on the road, I handed him my bag with the gun inside and he casually took it and stashed it under the car seat. I know I should have waited until it was safer to do so, but I did not want to be in possession of a weapon that could possibly end my life.
I remember him saying, "*baby girl! Are you okay? Thank you for looking after my gun,*" I

gave him a blank stare and looked away. I was the first one to be dropped off; I watched them drive off and gave a huge sigh. I was finally safe and home. I later found out that the men who were attacking us were members of a taxi association that controlled the taxies that collected people after work. The Nigerian driver was not registered with the association hence the scuffle. I also found out that on that night they followed him home and slashed his tires and banged up the windows.

After the incident, I questioned my safety around the Nigerian driver; that is when I was introduced to a new driver. He was a Zimbabwean, I hated the way he drove, he would tuck his head down changing the radio stations, when he could not find the right channel that suit his needs he would stretch over to the cubbyhole and look for his flash drive. I always felt that each night I rode with him would be my last night worse if the fidgeting wasn't going to kill us it was definitely going to be how he packed us the same one would pack cabbages. He would drive the Toyota Wish at a God forsaken speed, play the radio just as loud, and speak as loud as he could. He was proud of the fact that he could speak in the South African languages that most South African waiters spoke. The way he tried to accommodate; all his clients felt nothing close to good hospitality. I dreaded every night that I had to ride home in his car.

Chapter 9

My fear of Nigerians was so much that I couldn't be friends with them, let alone be in a romantic relationship with them; not that I wanted to be in one. I met Tim on one of my off days, I was busy learning how to cook prawns; they tasted so good the first time I ate them I just had to know how to make them and lucky for me my uncle had the tips. *Boil, boil, boil, and then fry.* After hours of boiling and then frying I went out with my cousin, she wanted to ride her bike and it was a bit too early to have supper. I walked slowly behind her, scrolling through my Facebook feed as she rode her bicycle around the complex. We passed by a house that had a bunch of Nigerians sitting on the verandah, I knew this by the way they were talking and of course their choice of clothes. I called out to my cousin to change the route because fear was slowly creeping up within me. She ignored my persistent yell until I decided to plant my face deep into my phone screen. She was already a few houses ahead, and I was too late to turn back.

"Hello!" one of the men shouted as I passed them. My knees trembled, I could not walk faster, and it felt as if my feet were dragging behind me. With my phone tightly secured in my hands, I glanced at them, gave a friendly but short smile, and replied under my breath; enough to avoid a conversation.

"Hie." I continued walking with my sight still fixated on the tiny blue screen.

"Why don't you join us, eeh?" another man who was lounged by the small flight of stairs, he had a glass that had golden brown liquid just two fingers from the bottom. I gave another short smile and shook my head. I tried to quicken my pace but it only made me walk funny.

They started talking in what I thought was Nigerian native tongue. I somehow took a deep breath and I found the strength to walk as fast as my legs could carry me. I finally caught up with my cousin who apparently was tired of riding and blamed me for slowing her down. We had supper and the night passed and the next day came, I cleaned the house and after I was done, I went to the store to get bread for breakfast. I was going to be working later that day so I needed change to pay for my taxi fare. When I reached the gate, I bumped into one of the men who were sitting and drinking.

"Hie, are you good?" he said. His accent was not like the other men he was with, neither did it sound Nigerian.

"Hie, yes I am, how are you?" I looked at my phone and turned down the song that was playing. I did not want to seem rude but at the same time did not want to have a long conversation with him.

"Are you going to PnP?" he asked.
"Yes." I did not know what else to say to him so I kept quiet.
"You like walking alone, I always see you on your phone with earphones plugged in." he smiled as he stared at me. I tried to avoid eye contact. Before I could say anything, he continued talking. *"I want to be your friend."* I was stunned by the way; he shoved that request in my face. It was not bad, but I did not have the space to accommodate new people in my life. When I was about to respond, he snatched my phone and punched in his number, saved it and called his phone so that he could save mine. I stood in awe, with my heart partially having an attack as I thought that he was stealing my phone.

I plugged my earphones into my ears as we parted ways. I could not believe the way he handled the whole situation, he radiated a dominating nature, which I did not like. I thought he was full of himself, *how could he just demand to be my friend and most importantly take my phone without my permission.* I convinced myself that I was not going to send him a text or call him, he did not give me a say in getting his number or being his friend. I quickly erased the lingering thoughts of him as I entered the shop and headed for the bread aisle, I picked up the white bread and saw eggs strategically placed next to the bread and decided to grab them too. The song that was playing on my playlist was rudely interrupted by an incoming phone call. I checked the caller ID and saw a name I did not quite recognize, I answered the call and moved to the back of the queue so that I avoid holding up the line.
"Just checking that you haven't blocked me, are you done yet I'm at the pool come join me." Again, his tone was commanding, it immediately put me off and declined his offer telling him that I had to prepare for work. I moved up the queue, slightly annoyed by the call I had received.
"*No chocolate today?"* the teller smiled as she asked me. She noticed that my morning shopping was one item short. Right then I realized that I had forgotten to take my eleven rand that was meant to cater for my chocolate addiction.
"*Not now maybe later, I didn't bring any money*." I smiled back. The checked out the items that I had bought and I walked out of the shop. Upon reaching the complex I saw Tim sitting by the pool area, he had some friends with him and I swore to myself that I was not going to go anywhere near them. I managed to avoid him that day, physically but he blew my phone up sending texts trying to make conversations with me and reluctantly I responded.

The back and forth texting made the distance that I had created between us grow smaller. I started to tolerate him and noticed that he was not that bad after all. In getting, to know him: Tim was a musician and a soccer player, and I had seen his music a number of times on the Trace music channel but snubbed it off thinking it could have been his look alike. It was until he told me that he was a singer that I suddenly realized that I used to listen to his music while cleaning. He was average height and had the stature of a soccer player, curved legs and a well looked after body. He was a little attractive but his attitude made me prefer him in the friend zone. During my friendship with Tim I made other friends, a Pedi girl called Thabang and a Zimbabwean girl called Gugu. We had so much fun taking walks to the mall and window-shopping, sometimes we would try on clothes, and shoes

as if we wanted to buy them and pretend that something had annoyed us and made us leave without doing the purchase. I almost had a fall out with Tim because of one of my new friend, he had invited me to a party at his place, as always I declined his offer; even though he had become my friend, I still did not trust him.
"*How could you say no to him he is a celebrity?*" Gugu asked me as we were walking to Thabang's house.
"*What does that have to do with me?*" I looked at her taking a selfie with her phone. She never missed an opportunity to take a photo.
"The guy obviously likes you and wants to spend time with you." She added, *"I have seen how he looks at you and you just ignore him. He is a soccer player Lizzy!"* she shoved her phone in her pocket and gave me a glare.
"*So what if he is a soccer player, I am busy?*" I took out my phone and texted a message to my mother and put my phone back in my pocket.
"*He has money, duh!*" she walked ahead of me and up the stairs to Thabang's door.
"*I don't want his money, and neither do I want him in any other way beside as friends.*" I checked my phone, Thabang walked out and we exchanged pleasantries.
"Thabang, can you believe that Lizzy said no to Tim's invite?" she told Thabang, who was quick to take my side.
"*So?*" she glared at her.
"*But its Tim?*" she cried. We walked down the complex street, not realizing that Gugu had made us walk in the direction of Tim's house.
"*Gugu, just tell Lizzy to get you an invite to his party. I know you want to go.*" Thabang and I broke out in laughter.
"*Yes Lizzy get me an invite, if you don't want to go.*" She begged. I could not believe that she was seriously considering going to the Nigerian party.
"*You will ask him yourself.*" I told her, and then she stopped walking. *"Okay, let's knock on his door and I will ask him."* She stood facing the entrance to Tim's house, and it looked deserted.

"Are you crazy? You purposely led us here." I screamed and walked away leaving them standing. Thabang followed behind me slowly, leaving Gugu standing in the driveway.
"Just leave her Lizzy." She said as she came up to me. *"I am not going to be involved in whatever she does; besides I have to get ready for work, will see you guys tomorrow."*
Thabang walked with me and we parted ways as she went to her house and we did not see Gugu the rest of that day.
Later that day, at work I was busy checking the reservations and matching them with the tables; my phone rang. I ignored it because Mr Black was standing by my post and I did not want to get in trouble with him. The phone stopped ringing, and I quickly finished what I was doing while thinking of a way to escape to the bathroom and attend to my phone.
"*Lizzy I need you to take an order to City Lodge, that runner is not back yet*." The opportunity I needed fell in my hands; without saying a word, in haste printed out the bill and dashed to the kitchen. I found the order ready and without thinking twice, I sped out the mall. I checked my phone the moment I was out of sight and I had missed Tim's

phone call twice. I texted him and he responded pissed at me, asking why I had given Gugu his number. I was stunned as I had not done such a thing, I told him about how she wanted to go his party and he emphasized that if I wasn't going to be there he was not going to give anyone else an invite. I apologized to him even though I knew that I was not in the wrong and continued with the City Lodge order. He later called me, apologized for scolding me, and told me that he had found out who had given out his number. Gugu's cousin who was also friends with Tim had given the number to Gugu.

He moved away some months later. I was partially thrilled that he was not going to keep nagging me to come over to his place, because when he relocated, I lost his contacts and lost communication with him.

Chapter 10

I missed my mother more than I did upon my initial arrival and felt much more alienated. I kept to myself more, and felt that being on my own was much better than being with other people. I would take long walks around the complex just to keep myself distracted from the thoughts in my head. Most of these times I would avoid my friends *Gugu and Thabang*; just to have time to myself. I remember during my walks; I would see complete families and wonder how mine went wrong; the feeling of being robbed was still etched in me even though years had passed after my father's death.

I found family at the restaurant, like Martha and Simon who would sneak a plate of chips or jalapeno slammers on to my delivery tray so that I can eat on my way back from a delivery. They were not exactly the void filler that I wanted but they made me feel visible. They were both from Zimbabwe; Martha was a Shona and was married to a Ndebele speaking man who was also a cook at the restaurant. At first, I thought that her husband was South African until I noticed how much they looked alike, then I thought that they were siblings; this was before I found out they were a couple. Simon was Kalanga, but spoke in Ndebele mostly and would try to speak to me in Shona. It was heartwarming to have people who spoke the same language as you did and spoke of the same things you knew from back home. Then there was Bra Isaac who was always at my rescue when rude customers sneer at me. Bra Isaac would take me to lunch and have me indulge in a bread and Maas combination and sometimes banana bread and a coke. Lunch with him meant I would never pay for anything, which made my pocket happy and meant I had extra cents to add to my education. Bra Isaac was Xhosa, short in stature and very light in complexion. His baldhead would shine through the well-lit restaurant, and would turn red whenever customers get on his nerves. He exuded my grandfather's qualities, I felt close to him as if I had known him for a longer period than this. He introduced me to old classics, like Teddy Pendergrass and Cece Wayans; I was already into Maxi Priest and Toni Rebel because they reminded me of my father. Through spending time with him, I noticed that he was an honest man; more honest that most of the people that I worked with. He would speak openly on his past behavior and give me life lessons from it. Whenever he saw girls my age partying and drinking, he would say, *"Sweetie, you are so young to be here. You should have a dream and don't die a waiter like the rest of us."* Bra Isaac's words would open my eyes and have me start to daydream of the person I wanted to be, but it was hard for me to find that person.

Sometimes the fact that I did not have a tertiary education background yet would bring me down and I would think that maybe I was destined to wiping tables and vomit off the floors each night. I would stand by the door at my post and watch the world pass me by. I loved the host shift much better than the runner one; it was much better than the black get up paired with a wet dishcloth and a dry one always ready for cleaning up other people's messes. Being ordered around usually got on my nerves, especially if that ordering was coming from people my age or younger than I was. I would wear a smile and pretend as if I was thrilled to be at their service. The more people mentioned that I was young to work in restaurants the more I lost interest in being there and the more I wanted something better for myself. Besides rumors of Xenophobia were circling around, a very scary time indeed. South Africans were not happy with foreigners taking up spaces in the work place, their frustration was understandable there were more Zimbabweans working in restaurants than South Africans; we had problems of our own and South Africa was everyone's escape. It could not be mine, no matter how hard I tried. I would go to my deliveries feeling scared even though where the restaurant was located was taxis away from the xenophobic action. As a precaution the managers took, I spent most of my night shifts at the restaurant while the other male runners took over the deliveries to the City Lodge. I was scared especially when I went home; I feared that the attackers would pounce at any moment.

One night on my delivery, I met a French-speaking couple; they had ordered our famous Garage burger and an ostrich burger. They came from Mali; the woman was quite friendly and bubbly while the man maintained a chilled vibe. The woman invited me in to her room; we were not allowed to do this but the other runner who trained me told me it was the only way to get the customers tipping, especially those booked at the lodge. I needed the tip so I said a little prayer under my breath and entered the room. I kept my smile planted on my face as I headed for the table that was located by the window. The husband was busy with a bunch of papers while sitting comfortably on the bed, I handed the woman the tiny bill folder and place the plates carefully on the table as she looked at the piece of paper lodged in the folder.

"*Babe, did you order a garage burger? What is that*?" she turned to me as waited for an answer from both her husband and me. I did not know when to respond, as the husband did not seem bothered, so I just blurted out an answer.

"*It's our signature burger it has an extra patty and melted cheese."* I had forgotten what was in the garage burger so I improvised with what I had seen while it was being made.

"*You said you wanted a burger, I ordered one"* the husband responded keeping his focus on the papers. Then they broke into in French, I knew what it was because I always wanted to learn it but never did. It suddenly became awkward in the room as I was not sure about what they were saying but the husband looked at me, smiled, and said something to his wife. I felt awkward standing before them and not knowing what they were discussing.

"How old are you dear?" the wife said as she grabbed her husband's wallet. "*I'm nineteen almost twenty*" I responded and glanced at the swipe machine, checking if the network was still available. They spoke in French again then turned to me again, "*Where are you from, you don't look South African?"* I was starting to feel uneasy; I wondered what they were talking about when they switched to French.

"*I'm from Zimbabwe*," I pressed a button on the swipe machine, hoping that it will make her realize that I was waiting for payment.

"*Oh! You could never tell through your accent. Are you not afraid though because of the*

attacks, surely it's not safe for you to walk at night?" he wore a worried look on her face. The way she put it was as if only Zimbabwean were being attacked by the South Africans. When I was about to respond to her, she took out some money and spoke, *"We are from Mali. Here on holiday but our second home is Durban."* I pulled the swipe machine to my chest as I realized that they were going to pay in cash.
"Oh! That is why you speak in French? It is French right?" I pretended as if I did not know.
"*Yes. You speak French*?" she inquired and retracted the money that was almost out of the wallet. *"No, but I love the language."* I responded, thought that if I remained friendly, it would earn me a larger tip.
"We would like you to help us with something dear, you seem like an intelligent young lady and you are beautiful and I hate to ask something like this in this manner." Her husband put down the papers, removed his spectacles, and placed them on the pillow close to him.
"*What do you need help with?"* I inquired, I thought maybe she wanted to pay her bill later or maybe bring another plate to them.
"*We need an egg; in fact, we need a surrogate*." I was stunned; I wore a constipated look as I watched her looking at the bill again and counting the money that was due and added two hundred Rands to the bill.
"Oh? I don't know if I know anyone who does that," I told her as I carefully placed the money in the bill folder and took a few steps towards the door. Fear nudged me on my side and my instincts kicked in telling me to escape.
"*No sweetie, we want you to be our surrogate, I know it is short notice and we barely know you but we like you. And we will pay and manage all your expenses."* She explained and the man sat up, he called his wife who turned her head in his direction and they spoke in French again.
"*Okay, listen. Take my business card and think about this; call me whenever you are ready*."
I walked out of the room feeling confused. I took out my phone and googled surrogacy. The amount of money surrogates made had me thinking about the offer they had on the table. I was going to pay for my studies and at the same time be able to look after my mother. This meant I could be able to leave South Africa within nine months. I had never been pregnant but I thought it would be an easy thing to do and I would be helping someone and myself at the same time. I contemplated deeply about this offer; I was already struggling with paying my fees this was going to be a foolproof plan to get all my affairs in order. A call to my mother made me think otherwise, she told me of the complications involved with pregnancy and I for one had always been afraid of being pregnant before marriage. I would be a disappointment in the eyes of my uncles, I thought. I never called them, they never looked for me; they must have picked up the hint that I was not interested, truth is I was scared.

Calls to my mother had become a ritual.
Anytime I felt alone *which, was all the time,* I would call her up and chat, talking about everything that hurt me. Sometimes I would do so under the tree next to the pool and the house lights in sight. I would take out my burger or jalapeno slammers and have my 'lunch' *I would have it late, at midnight or one a.m. depending on what time I would have arrived home, because it would have been too busy for me to have it at the correct lunch*

time and secretly indulge on the food. It is not that I did not want to share my food with them, it was the only one thing that I had that belonged to me, and I was not restricted or limited.

My secret meals under the watchful eye of the moon. I would change up my spot because of a cat that also took refuge under the tree and I would sit under the stairs. This new spot was perfect, dark, and quiet. I would sit there talk to my mom while I ate, she knew about my thing. She knew that I did not want putting people in a complicated situation, *whatever that meant*. Having my secret meals, saved 'them' the costs, and I was not a burden anymore. That is what I thought.
I lost a burger once, at my new spot. I remember that burger, a well-done beef patty, smothered in pepper sauce and the chips dunked in a creamy chili-cheese sauce. A weird combination, but I was craving for it so bad the whole day. I had just finished talking to my mother, and I remember taking my time, savoring the flavors on my taste buds. The sweet basting sauce on the beef patty did not over power the kick that the pepper sauce had; it was all just perfect. On this day I had knocked off a little earlier than most days, it must have been around eleven p.m. I heard footsteps coming down the stairs, and because I did not want my 'family' finding out about my secret, I dumped the whole takeaway container in the bin that was close to me. I waited a few minutes and then went up the stairs; only to find out that it was our upstairs neighbor coming down for a smoke, *it must have been his secret too.*

Chapter 11

Sometimes I ate at work.
Hiding at the far end corner of the non-smoking section. Table one was a twelve sitter that looked like it could cater for a much bigger party. People did not like to sit there; it was too dark and had an eerie atmosphere. The waiters said it was haunted, I never believed them, and it was too plain to be haunted. It did not look like any ghost would want to stick around; it was more lonely than haunted. Anyone sitting there would be cut off from the rest of the restaurant.
I liked it; the perfect place for someone like me, someone who did not fit in. It was home. Mr Black or Mr Nick would order me something, a pepper burger, mushroom burger, or a cheeseburger. Sometimes I would swap the cheese for monkey gland sauce. I only did it once or twice *I do not quite remember;* I could not bring my mind to accepting that it was not Monkey organs.
I would sit in the corner, hidden from the cameras because I did not want Ms.Cee catching me. Quickly I would gobble down the burger and the chili cheese fries. Oh, how I loved chili cheese fries; these were potato chips, fried then dunked in a chili cheese sauce. The sauce maker, in a pot melted the cheddar and mozzarella cheese and when it was a porridge like texture, he poured in the hot chili sauce. He would later pour the mixture in a bain-marie and kept it warm so that it does not stiffen up. This was not the first time I would hide while eating, I did this when I was still a runner. The kitchen staff would add me to the lunch list even though runners were not allowed to eat food prepared in the restaurant. Taffy *the other runner* and I would squeeze ourselves in a corner, next to the heavy-duty dishwasher and share a plate of sadza. Sometimes he would leave me some on the plate after having a few morsels, *you are the baby, you need to grow* he would say and stand as a decoy, washing forks and knives. When I was done, he would leave one batch so that the camera could record me getting the utensils out. I am sure the bosses knew, they just never said anything. One waiter was caught though, eating an avocado in our corner. I do not blame her, she was pregnant probably she suddenly craved for it.

A part of me thinks that the other waiters might have been jealous of me; maybe Taffy was, when I was promoted to the door manager. He did not change his behavior towards me, for me to think that he could have been jealous, but I know I would feel some type of peevish way if the new kid got a promotion before me. One waiter accused me of using some supernatural power, voodoo maybe... *your N'anga is amazing young girl,* he would say as I walked around checking if tables were set properly. *What do you mean? I do not have a N'anga,* I would respond. A little taken aback, how could he think that I would do something like that? *You just got here and now you are assigning us where to work. That is some serious voodoo… give me some,* he would nag, chewing a squashed bun he would have stolen in the kitchen during delivery. I walked away from him. Irritated, he did not want to hear anything that I was saying. He was convinced that I had used some kind of magic to get the promotion. This would not the last time he would nag me about sharing some of my *magic.*

Chapter 12

I found my second escape, a shop that sold gems and energy stones. I was walking around the Montecasino Mall during my lunch hour; Bra Isaac was off on that day and so were the other people that I had grown close. Something on that day was urging me to be on my own, I just wanted a walk and to find something that meant something to me. I was somehow on a mission to find my purpose on earth. I came across the gem shop; the scents of essence sticks and scented candles that were burning in the shop lured me and Lady Peace revealed herself.
The bustling traffic in my head went quiet, as if it were a pause, waiting to see what was coming. The moment I entered through the doors of the shop, the energy of the whole place embraced me in a protective cocoon. Filled with awe and a bit scared of the people that were in the shop who were also customers; adventurously I moseyed around, looking at the tiny stones that exuded so much love. I thought the shop owners would chase me away. Maybe it was because I felt like a reject amongst other humans and I thought this welcoming place was going to spit me out as well.

I was drawn to a stone, a blue turquoise; I just had to buy it as it called out to me. The woman in the shop was so excited to sell me that stone; *I see someone was chosen.* I smiled at her and wondered what she meant by that. *Yes. I just liked the color.* The turquoise stone shaped like a tooth, a dog's tooth to be precise and not too much detail on it. It was perfect *something not loud enough to draw attention from the thieves.* It hung on my neck from a black thread; *even better thieves would not want anything like that.* I thought. She told me about the healing powers the stone had. I believed her. I was getting used to these things; the supernatural and the spiritual. I had always been an open-minded human. She asked if I wanted a free reading for me, and brought out tarot cards, after I had accepted. She asked me to pull out a card and when I did, she smiled at the card that I had pulled out. It had an image of a golden chalice. She told me it meant good things coming my way. *When?* I smiled back and thanked her while wrecking my head wondering about my big break.

Did your grandfather give you that stone, what is that? It looks like a tooth. The nagging waiter said, standing next to me. There was not a time I did not see him eating, I had nicknamed him Mr. Ibu a character in one of the Nigerian movies I used to watch; come to think of it, he looked exactly like him, potbellied and dark in complexion and he stuffed bread in his pockets, just like Mr. Ibu. I would look at him and wonder what his wife looked like. *Why is it on a thread, black thread? Is that your muthi?* He would blabber irritatingly; I swear I had a mind to slap him across the face. I couldn't, he was my

senior; I would slow down the traffic to his section, put reserve signs on three maybe four tables that would definitely teach him not to mess with me.
I had the power and I was going to use it...

***

The Human Resources course that I was doing gave me some kind of hope, the kind of hope that finds you walking barefoot on shards of glass and smiling through the pain. I saved up the little change that I got from the customers at the lodge and when it was enough for fees payment, I would do so and in turn get my course work; it was a perfectly laid out plan... *and so I thought.* I found myself knee deep in debt, the money I got from the restaurant was just not enough. I decided to search for a second job, one I would do during the day on a part time basis. It had to be something that paid double if not more than what I was getting. I considered that surrogate offer I got while on my delivery shift; it was pointless, I did not have their numbers anymore. Griefful, I surfed through the internet looking for something that could help me pay my way and ended up on Facebook. It was not an ideal place to look for a job, but there were many job posts on it. I found one job call, it seemed quite easy and did not have much requirements needed: LOOKING FOR LADIES AGED 18 TO 35, MUST BE GOOD LOOKING. I paused over the post and wondered what of job it was. I scrolled through the post's owner and everything seemed legit. I the decided to send him a message after gathering enough courage and lucky for me he responded. I was thrilled.
He introduced himself and he seemed to be interested in hiring me for the job. He stopped texting for a while and moments later, he sent a text; *I looked at your profile and you will do.* Confused about his remark, I asked him, *what does the job description entail?* His remark continued to roam in my head I wanted to brush it off because I needed the job but I could not I wanted to know what he meant. He said to me *don't worry you will be perfect for the job, just go the address I gave you in Sandton and see the man in charge.* I do not remember the name of the man I was supposed to see for the interview. I asked him again, *okay! By the way, what did you say the job was, because I do not have any experience in acting or modeling?* He budged and gave me a little information, *it is like an online chat room, it pays about thirty thousand Rands a month, and all you have to do is keep the client interested in talking to you. You get a laptop and a room and you set up your own hours.* The description sounded a little too good to be true. I thought 30k for just talking to people what was the catch. I suddenly started feeling scared. I wanted a second job to pay off my school debt but it was just too sketchy for me. I told the person that I was going to be available for the interview and as soon as he was offline, I blocked him on the platform. I went to work later that day feeling scared of the conversation I had just had. Days later, I saw a post on Facebook about a girl who had gone to the same address I was supposed to go to and she was raped by the people I was supposed to meet. I was stunned and terrified; *it could have been me,* I thought.

Chapter 13

My third escape, a huge isolated park with green scenery and beautiful boulders that stood at each of the corners sort of enclosing the park in. I would sit by the pond located on the western side of the park and watch a family of ducks waddle peacefully across it. There I would flip through my thoughts and meditate on each one of them. Thoughts of home would flood my head and in an instant, I would feel as though I was close to home. The footpaths would give the illusion of my way home, and I would imagine seeing my mother and father waiting for me at the end of the pathway. Sometimes I would only see my father, smiling as though he had been waiting for me to come home, the moment would be rudely interrupted by a rustle in the grass, and it would give me a scare thinking that it was a snake or something worse. Sometimes I would wish that whatever that was rustling would take me and not leave a trace of me. No one would miss me right. I was already invisible.

I remember the hypnotizing water reeds on the other side of the pond, a luscious green tuft dancing slowly for the calm wind as it brushed against them. I closed my eyes and felt a cool feather touch on my face followed by a gentle blow slowly bringing me back to my surroundings. I had found a nice spot there, secluded and quiet; nothing was going to compete with the noise that was in my head, nothing was going to disturb me thinking. It ticked all the boxes, the perfect spot to disappear. I wanted to be far away from everything. I felt at home hidden by the dainty green reeds and tall grass bordering the pond. Nature accepted me just as I was, I did not have to change myself or tweak a few edges to be perfect. She listened to me, sometimes I did not have to talk, we would just stare at each other, and she would show me stuff; A family of ducks, a weird colored leaf, or a strange carving on the tree trunks and looking at all these things made me feel that being different was good. The feeling never lasted as long as I wanted it to, it scurried away like frightened rats whenever my alarm went off.
Time to put on a fake smile and pretend that the tears in my eyes were the sparkle, that everyone expected me to have. Just because I had to be grateful, blend in, be like them, and be them. No one ever told me that directly, it was in the air waiting for me to breathe it in. Every time I tried it or forced myself to be, I lost a part of my self.

The day I lost my first job, I was coming from a long walk after spending my moments in the park. I took a shower at around lunchtime getting myself ready for my 5pm shift. Then my phone rang, when I looked at the caller ID it was my boss. She asked me if I was already on my way to work, I was stunned thinking I had enough time to get to work and thought maybe I forgot about a shift time change.
I am getting ready to come there; I will be there in no time. I responded confidently and wondering why she suddenly had to check on me.

You do not need to come in today Liz. She paused; I was taken aback and thought that maybe she was letting her son take my shift for some reason. She always did if he needed pocket money and I would be a penny short. *I have been informed that the home affairs department is doing an inventory on documented workers, and seeing that you are not one of them, you might be arrested.* I went silent, I did not quite get what she was saying but somehow knew that this was it; I was losing my job. *Unless you are able to get a permit, I cannot help you, I am sorry dear, but I have to let you go.*
Ms Cee broke the bad news to me. And it tore me apart. This was all I had. This job was all had in South Africa that meant something to me.
Apparently, the home affairs department was dealing with the xenophobic attacks by deporting the illegal immigrants. Surely, they were saving our lives but at the same time ruining it. How was I going to raise money for a twelve thousand rand permit? I could barely pay my twelve thousand rand school fees in one payment. My heart broke; my stars were not aligning in my favor. I hung up the call and flung myself on the bed. *Was this, the good thing that tarot reader saw?*

I cried; even though it was pointless, I cried. That job was the only thing that I had, that felt like family; a place filled with misfits and as if it was a puzzle, I was the missing piece, the only place I found peace and the only place that actually welcomed me. After hours of shedding tears, I came out of the room and saw my uncle in the living room watching TV; *oh, you are still here, I thought you left already.* He said as he flicked through the channels. I told him about the misfortune that had befell me, tears stinging my eyes forcing themselves out. He was so calm about it and I did not understand why, somehow I expected more affection and remorse, but he did not feel the same connection I had with the place. He told me, *it happens, and just had to move on from it. You will find another job.*
I needed a break, from everything; with the little money, I had saved up. I thought I would go back home to Zimbabwe and maybe reboot myself or forget about South Africa. I did not know what to do or where to start looking for another job, of course, it should have been the first option, but I still did not have the money to get a permit. I wanted to throw in the towel.

It was almost Christmas, and I was going to be home alone. My uncle and his family had plans for their own getaway and I knew that I was not included in their plans, I made mine to go back home. The trip home was exactly what I needed, seeing my mom and her smiles would warm me up, and soon I would forget all my worries.
When I arrived home, I did not want to go back to South Africa, that dreaded place was hell for me, but I was not one to give up. I tried not to cry before my mother, I wanted her to be proud of me and I wanted to prove to my uncle that I was not a quitter.

I visited my Aunt during 'my break'; I could say we spent most of the holiday at her house, my mother loved spending time at her brother's, and I felt at home with his family. They lived just a few streets away from our place. My Aunt's bubbly personality always made me forget my worries. She had the gift too; maybe that is why I connected with her. I recall when I first saw her healing a client; it was during one of our visits and when we suggested that we left her to do her work and she refused and asked us to stick around. A part of me thinks she wanted me to see what I could possibly become if I accepted my gift. She knew about the dreams and the voices, I told her.

Now this woman was sitting on the floor in my aunt's sitting room, she had a doek tightly wrapped on her head and another wrapper tightly around her waist. My aunt came out of her room, spotting her apostolic regalia, a red garment, and a white head wrap. I remember feeling a bit uneasy upon setting my eye on her. I thought *this was not me; I was not going to dress in that get up. Seeing her, helped me make my decision fast, I did not want the gift anymore.* She said some prayers; her Shona was deep, not like the way she usually spoke. I could only pick up a few words and I could pick out that the woman was facing trouble with goblins that were making her sick. I watched my aunt taking lemons and coarse salt, and rubbing it all over the woman's back and shoulders. The woman started shrieking, *obviously from the stinging lemon and salt*; but my aunt said that the goblins were reacting to the lemon and salt combo. After what seemed to be an hour, she stopped squirming, screaming and she became still. I exchanged glances between my aunt and the inanimate woman staring into nothingness; it was a scary sight, thoughts started to fly through my head *was this the life waiting for me?* I saw more of these healing sessions, each different from the last and they all gave me a fright. I remember telling my mother that I did not want the gift, '*I wanted to be like other girls*' I cried. *Who would want to be near a weird freak like me*? I took it upon myself to block the gift; I would ignore any dreams, messages, and signs until it leaves me alone, and I had to leave first. I had to go back and finish what I had started; reluctant. Yes. But a choice is something I felt like I did not have.

Chapter 14

I returned to South Africa, and so did the dreams and the voices. I thought I was actually going crazy. I would have vivid dreams that shook me and sometimes left me scared. I got myself accustomed to essence sticks; I would burn the sage and lavender sticks to ward off nightmares that were availing every night, someone said they help banish bad dreams and evil scares. My uncle blamed the horror movies that I loved to watch, but these were too far off to be a vivid imagination. Like this one time, I was woken up by sounds of drums banging and loud roars of lions. I listened hard, knowing that we stayed far from any park, or zoo that had lions it concerned me. I closed my eyes and meditated on the sounds I was hearing, and then I heard a voice telling me that I was going to hear some bad news coming from home. I mentioned this to my uncle asking him if he had heard anything, to which he protested blaming my vivid imaginings. When I told my mother, she sighed, as would person tired of dealing with bad news.
Days after the weird experience, we received news that my grandmother's sister had passed away.

I started job hunting, and it was hard. I did not know where to start and the only place I knew was Montecasino because I never had time to go places and because I did not like going out. I was well acquainted with the areas that surrounded Montecasino but I did not want to be anywhere, near the place. It's what I do, if something hurt me I distance myself from it, it's easier that way and as long as the thing that hurt me is bottled up I can move on and do whatever that follows next. There was a mall near the new place my uncle had moved to, I took a walk to it; one because I had to save money and two walking had become a part of me. I went in and out of restaurants dropping my CVs that only mentioned the only job experience I had. Every place that I went to was a dead end and the more I walked the further I became getting to my destination. I would get home exhausted and depressed; my aunt's silence would make me feel worse. I started to feel like I was burdening them.

I wandered further to an area that was known as Brightwater Commons, it was another mall filled with shops and restaurants; I did the CV dropping game again. My uncle had told me about the place and by myself, I went on a mission to find it. The walk to the place was tiring and hard, even though I had taken a taxi half way to the place; the sun was blazing hot and I was hungry. When I was about to give up, I saw Spur, a restaurant that was famous for its steaks and ribs, I entered the restaurant and asked to see the manager. The smell of the fried chips and tasty meat made my tummy growl, but it was pointless as the only money I had on me was meant for job searching expenses; food was just some luxury. The manager came; I introduced myself to him, smiling as hard as I could trying hard to hide hunger on my face. I handed him my CV and cracked my

knuckles as I watched him going through it.
Oh, so you worked at Montecasino. Why did you leave that place? He asked me the question I dreaded the most, how was I was going to explain to him that I did not have a permit to work and now, I had a fake one plastered on my passport. He stared at the photocopy of my passport that was attached to my CV, I was relieved that he did not ask for the original passport; I feared that he was going to tell that it was faked.
Getting the fake permit was the second extreme thing that I had ever done in my life. The first being in possession of a gun, even though it was for a short time. I was accompanied by my uncle to one of his friends who pawned my tablet for the money that would suffice to get the permit. I took a taxi to Braamfontein by myself an area I only knew passing by from my trips to and from Zimbabwe. I was instructed to go to a salon that was located opposite an Engen petrol station. I remember clutching my purse that had my passport and three thousand Rands close to my chest as I widened my eyes looking for the salon. I dialed the number of the person that I was going to meet, and he instructed me to wait for him inside the salon once I had arrived. The Salon was a tiny room sandwiched between two buildings, one a clothing store and the other a garage with panel beaters busy at work. I slithered in to the tiny shop and inside was a chaos, hairdressers and weave pieces everywhere and the smell of burning hair suffocating the place. On the opposite side, phone technicians busy fixing their clients' phones. I spoke to one woman who thought that I had come to get my hair done, I asked her about the man in question, and she gave me a seat while I waited. After a few uncomfortable moments the man came, he did not seem like an under handed person at all. He asked me to give him the passport and he left the salon. The wait was terrifying, thoughts of robbers coming in the salon or worse police busting in and arresting everyone for dealing in fake permits. My heart was pounding, the jokes that were being told felt like torture. After a painful wait, he came back with my passport with a new work permit. It had everything a legit permit had; it looked like the real thing. I gave him the money and made my way home, with a pounding chest knowing that I had done something illegal.

Chapter 15

Now I was staring at the Spur manager, he was waiting for my response.
I have moved and the new place is far from Montecasino, I felt my mouth drying up. He cleared his throat and asked me another question that triggered fear in me.
Do you have a work permit? I wanted to say no, because I was afraid that if I said yes, he would ask to see it and he was going to notice that it was faked. I forced a smile and said yes and in anticipation waited for him to ask to see it. I could not say no, because that would mean I would not get a job. He did not ask to see my passport; he closed the pages of my CV and folded it. He then told me to return for training at 3pm. I was thrilled; I finally had a positive response. I had to change my clothes, wear a blue jean, and black t-shirt; excitedly I dashed out of the mall and made my way to the taxi rank so that I would not be late. While I was busy looking for transport to go home, I realized that I had run out of money; I could only get home for a change, but returning to the Spur restaurant was going to be difficult. I started walking while pondering about my predicament, I had found a job that was going to make my life easier but I could not pay my way to and from work.

I came up to another place that had quite a few restaurants, I thought to drop in the last CV had even though I had already found a job, I do not know why I was doing it as the predicament I was already facing was going to be the same if I got the job here too. Some friendly men at a restaurant referred me to an Indian restaurant that had just opened; their restaurant did not employ any female waiters.

Tired and starved I went across the road to the Indian place called 1860 Indian Cuisine; the waiters there were all bubbly and excited to see me as if they knew me. I asked to see the manager of the place; it was a young Indian woman they referred to as Avinash. She was a young Indian woman, with long brown hair. Avinash had beautiful big brown eyes that complimented her hair and her tan skin tone. Her petit body made her jeans fit her perfectly as if they were custom made for her. She had a welcoming smile as she took me to a table at the far end of the tiny restaurant that had about five tables inside and two just outside at the entrance. I introduced myself and she looked at the last document I was left with, she jumped up in excitement as she read my birth date, *Oh my word! Your birthday is the same as mine;* I smiled not knowing if I should respond to her, hunger was nibbling at my stomach.
She looked at my clothes, *are you able to get a change of clothes? Do you stay far from here?* She inquired. I looked at her, and as I was about to reply her she intervened, we *need waiters, and you are perfect.* She stopped and paged through my CV to the last page.
I do not stay far from here. Not wanting to miss this opportunity, I lied through my teeth.
I called my uncle who happened to be in the same area as I was in and asked him if he could pick me up. I took a quick change and my uncle offered me a ride back to the

restaurant; he was picking up his wife. Along the way with my aunt in the car, With unmatched enthusiasm, I told her about the job I had finally found. I texted my mother who in turn was thrilled and thankful. She said prayers for me and like any concerned mother; she asked how I was getting to work and the time I was going to knock off. I could feel her excitement through her texts and a warm feeling graced my heart. Even though I confided in her about everything that happened to me in South Africa, I did not tell her about the moving out conversation. I figured that I would quickly finish my studies and move out well before I could step on anyone's toes.

There I was, in my black jeans tightly fastened as I had drastically lost weight and my black t-shirt that revealed my neckline that was skeletal. Avinash introduced me to another Indian who seemed to be the owner of the restaurant. I had applied for the waiter position but the owner was distracted and he sent me to the kitchen to start my first day. I was introduced to the assistant chef who immediately handed me a pocket of onions to start chopping. Eyes teary I went through the onions, the knife taking bits and pieces of my fingertips. I was not used to chopping anything especially at restaurant speed. The hours dragged along as I met with other new employees and listened to them narrating away about their encounters while on the job hunt. I did not know them; I did not want to lose my new job over talking and not working.

I was happy to have a job, I could pay my fees and resume school, and I could send some money to my mother; it was all that was important to me, not that she ever asked me for any money. It was not much, but I made sure I put aside a hundred rand from my tips while I was at the Gourmet and secretly hide it in either a toothpaste box that would be inside a small package I would give my uncle when he went on his visits to Zimbabwe. Now that I had a job, I would resume all this and so I thought. The pressure in the kitchen was too much for me, I kept on slicing bits of my fingertips with the knife I was using as the orders kept coming in.
I remember the hours dragging away; I did not have lunch that day as I had been walking the whole day looking for a job. I nibbled on the pieces of carrots as I chopped them and the scraps of cucumber that were left behind. The others I was working with seemed strong as if they had feasted on a filling meal and some had money; they would slip away to the KFC restaurant that was next door to buy a burger or two. I did not have money so I depended on the scraps to carry me through the day. We were told to stop chopping by the Indian head chef, who ordered me and three other girls to start washing the dirty dishes. While we were half way through the million plates, I could not feel my back and feet. I was a few minutes away from quitting. We emptied the sink using 20-liter buckets that once contained cooking oil, as the buckets of water weighed me down I felt tears rolling to the back of my eyes. I could not cry, I had to toughen up; I needed this job and there was no time for me to be a crybaby.

After hours of gruesome hard labour, the day was finally over. I started to wonder where I was going to get transport to take me home. The clock had struck midnight, hunger was gnawing at my tummy I could have sworn that my stomach was turning against me. I called the private cab driver that used to take me from Montecasino to my uncle's place. I stood outside the Domino's Pizza restaurant, since they still had they had their lights on and it seemed safer than the outside area of my work place. He came after an hour or two I was shivering, scared and all alone. As he drove me home, he kept on complaining about the distance he had to drive to get to me. I was too tired to listen to his whining. I finally arrived home, exhausted. I called my mother telling her that I had arrived home; I knew that she probably had not fallen asleep and was waiting for my call. We spoke for a little while as she asked about my day at work. I did not want to worry her, I kept the information of my day as fun as I possibly could though it was a definite day from hell. After the call I went up the stairs unlocked the door; everyone was sleeping; of course, I was not expecting anyone to be up by 2am. I was still hungry but I could not eat, I did not bother looking if there was any food left for me. I went straight to bed, and then insomnia hit and the conversation that happened in the car earlier that day started to replay. I started to wonder what could have caused them to suggest that I move out, it was not a bad idea, I was bound to start living on my own soon enough, but I felt like it was sprung on me. I had been told that my salary would be three thousand Rands. This was because I was working in the scullery section; I sat up on the bed and started to calculate how I would split the money. I was going to pay back the one thousand rand I owed my uncle even though I owed him five hundred Rands more, then I was going to pay another thousand to the college towards my three thousand rand debt and the last thousand was going to be for transport to and from work until my next pay date. Silently, my tears flowed down my cheeks, everything seemed to be weighing down on my shoulders, and it was only my second year in South Africa. I was trying to hold on but my grip was loosening, and I was feeling useless. I zoned out as my wet pillow soothed the headache that was looming.

Chapter 16

My new bosses needed all of the staff at 6am. I had to be early even though I was still exhausted; I had no other option. I left home before anyone else was awake; I remember feeling drained and more exhausted than the previous day. The second day of my new job started off on a good note, the bosses were friendlier than the previous day and the assistant chef made breakfast for the kitchen staff; so working was a breeze. I warmed up to the other girls that I chopped vegetables with; we became more acquainted after knowing that we were all from Zimbabwe. That inexplicable feeling that came with knowing that the person you came across or sitting next to was Zimbabwean came back. We would chat in vernacular as we chopped the vegetables and anything the head chef wanted. The pain of chili pepper seeds jumping into our eyes and the huge blades slicing bits of our fingertips along with the onions, cucumbers, tomatoes, and potatoes was some of the things we had to go through for the sake a few Rands. I knew what I was working towards and a little pain was not going to put me down.

The days went by and I slowly withered with them. I lost weight drastically and the only way to hide it was layering up on trousers and wearing oversized tops. It would have seemed that I had lost weight way before working at 1860, but I only noticed it after I suffered from a tummy ache for almost a week. My stomach took time to adjust to the curry that was served to us during lunchtime. The issue of my weight became known to me when I had a conversation with the head chef who was impressed by my chopping skills I had gained.
"*You are getting pretty good at your cutting skills*," he said as he lit a cigarette lounging himself on the artificial water fountain that was being installed on the patio.
"*Thank you sir,*" I responded. I noticed that his eyes were fixated on me and made me feel uncomfortable.
"*If you keep at it, I will teach you how to make curry,*" he took a long pull of his professionally rolled cigarette and shook of the ashes into the empty pond.
"*I would like that very much sir; Blessing is already teaching me how to make rotis.*" I thought if I mention my private lessons with the other chef it would get me moved to the cooking section or maybe out of the kitchen and to the front of house where I was more comfortable working. I loved the girls I was teamed with on cutting vegetables, but my fingers could not take the knife's kisses anymore. They were starting to look like the fingers of the dead bodies found in crime dramas like NCIS.
"*You know Selina?*" he threw the tiny cigarette bud that was in between his fingers over the balcony as he asked.
"*No I haven't met her yet,*" I responded trying to make sense of how we moved from talking about the kitchen to a person named Selina. While I was busy thinking and

chopping the owner and manager Billy came through from the kitchen door and threw a bunch of keys he had at Nathan- the head chef.
"Yo Bobby, doesn't she look like Selina," he spoke so fast I barely put together what he said. Bobby looked at him puzzled and looked at me; he shrugged his shoulders and walked away. Bobby did not speak much, at one point I thought that he did not know any English until one day I heard him talking to some people on the phone. He was average height and kept a clean haircut. His complexion was caramel toned a bit lighter than Nathan was and he was buff credit to the regular visits to the gym. Unlike Nathan, his love for food was not only visible in the way he prepared his dishes. He was not overweight but had a well-toned body probably because of gym as well. He had a tiny potbelly that showed when he removed his heavy chef jacket. His complexion was darker than the other Indian owners I had seen come to check out the restaurant. He had tattoos running throughout his arm; they all had tattoos similar ones that too. A part of me thought they were in a gang, not just because of the tattoos but because of the secret gatherings, they would have in dark corners. Surely, they must have been discussing about the restaurant and the club but something was sinister about the way they did it.

After he told me that I looked like 'Selina if only I had more flesh on the bones and longer hair', it troubled me. I started noticing how most of my clothes if not all them were not fitting me. I had no choice but to wear multiple trousers underneath the main trouser that I was going to wear to work just to cover up. Had I not done that my jeans looked as if someone was pulling them down each time I walked. I could not afford a new wardrobe so this was my only go to option, otherwise I would look like a hanger draped in clothing. Now that Nathan had aired it out, I wondered if he had noticed the unusual number of clothing I wore. This started to wear down my self-esteem and I avoided people more than I did before; preferred the background.

I tried many things to cover up my situation, I relaxed my hair, and with the chocolate brown hair color that I had dyed in made it worse, I looked like a sick person. I started seeing cheekbones that I never had protruding on both sides of my face and my once succulent cheeks sunk in and so did my eyes; I was the human version of the corpse bride. Each day I was reminded how skinny I was by the way people looked at me, I felt as if they were staring at me and at the verge of sending me to a hospice or worse rehab. I began hating my life and myself.

I remember one night when I had knocked off from work, Alex my previous driver had stopped picking me up due to the distance. I had no one to hike with because my colleague who were on duty that day stayed in Diepsloot, which was completely the opposite direction to where I was going. As I watched everyone getting into taxis and cars, I started to wonder how I was going to get home. At this time the only option I could think of was calling my uncle and ask if he could pick me up, he responded by suggesting that I try standing by the traffic lights and waving down security cars that passed by. His car was not working, I remember hanging up the call slightly disappointed and stressed. I looked at the place he had directed me, and I noticed that the place was dark and secluded. It was definitely not a safe option for me. I walked across to the

restaurants on the other side of the road; I approached the restaurant that had waiters who referred me to 1860. They were still serving customers, their side of the road was busier than where I was, and I was becoming scared standing by myself. As I walked towards the restaurant, I saw a man who was walking fast towards me. I clutched my purse that contained my passport and my thirty-one rand meant for my transport home, he saw how frightened I was and warned me shouting at the top of his voice.
"If you clutch your bag like that, we will think that you have money and mug you," he laughed and walked past me. My heart was pounding, I was certain that this man was one of Tsotsis. I moved to clearer and well-lit restaurant, it was quite busy and the traffic there guaranteed my safety. I started questioning my reasons for being in a country that clearly had no room for me. I looked at families that sat at the tables having fun, sharing stories and I thought of my broken family; my father was gone and I left my mother for a god-forsaken place in search for money. I went through my phone, looking for someone I could call to pick me up as it was getting late. I called Alex who ignored my calls and then the Nigerian driver who used to pick me up while I was working at Montecasino; he was available only after three or four hours. It seemed I was going to be stuck. Then I remembered the architect, he worked in Randburg and stayed in Fourways. It was on the same route as where I stayed. I called him and hoped that he would be available or out parting as usual and he was; he told me to wait for him where I was and he would come get me. I remember feeling relieved knowing someone was coming to my rescue. As I sat on a concrete slab in the parking lot, I started to think if I was ever going to be rescued from the hellhole I was in. I know I had so many chances to leave and I snubbed all of those chances all for one reason, to give my mom and myself a better chance at life. At this moment it seemed as though all my efforts were being thrown in the bin; I looked like a skeleton and probably a few steps towards my grave.

My hero for the night came; it was late, as most restaurants had closed. He parked his car in the parking lot and sounded his horn to alert his presence. This was the second time I was seeing him, we had maintained contact from our first encounter at Molly's Bar. I sat in the passenger seat and suddenly felt uncomfortable; it was as if I had just realized that he was a stranger. Thoughts of what he might do to me started to rummage through my head. I would steal glances at him, to see if he would do anything untoward. I remember him focused on the road as he spoke about how his work was demanding. His dark toned skin glistened in the car, reflecting the streetlights that shone through it. His voice as he spoke commanded authority it sent mixed messages as one point I felt safe and the next I felt as though I was in total danger. I texted my mother, she asked me if I trusted the valiant knight. All I wanted was to get home safely. I recall Dan asking if he could take me out for a drink where we had first met because it was closer to his house, I was exhausted, and I did not trust him; I found it best to decline his offer_ politely. When we were close to my place, I gave him the directions to the complex where I was staying. Bubbles of relief popped within me as I saw him take the exact turns that I told him to take. We arrived home, and as I walked away from the car and into the gate, he slowly backed-up his car as if he was making sure I got into the house safely. I phoned my mother, informing her of my arrival.

Chapter 17

I worked at a club for one night and swore never to do it for as long as I lived. We had been working since the morning at the restaurant and around eight in the evening, Bobby chose Melody, myself and another girl I seem not to remember her name. We were given a can of Redbull each, so that we do not fall asleep on the job. We were briefed on how we were going to work, and we were assigned to our sections. I was by the entrance, Melody was working the side where there was the stripper pole, and the other girl was given a section next to mine. Slowly people flooded the place and the noise grew louder, I could not keep up with the people who had ordered their drinks, one moment they would be by the bar and the next, near the toilets. The girls and I would alternate sections just to make the work easy and most importantly bearable; moreover, we were hoping to get tips. We got none, except for a hard time running after drunk customers as if they were toddlers. I remember being exhausted around 11 p.m. and watching Selina and her sister leave made me wish I could leave as well, but it was unfortunate that I was not related to the owners. Thinking that we were about to close, we saw more customers coming in; I recall Melody asking Jimmy, the one who was responsible for deliveries, about the time the club was going to close. He laughed in his high-pitched voice and told her *buckle up it's still a long ride.* My feet were killing me; it was as if my upper body had dislodged itself from the lower part. I forced myself to move about, as I was slowly dosing off; I went into the tiny kitchen with a tray of glasses and noticed a vast number of dirty glasses in the sink. I decided to wash the glasses as a way to catch a breath from the constant nagging. Four hours later, the noise subdued, the customers had staggered away, and we were yet to follow.

We did not know where to get transport home, we begged Bobby to give us a lift. He was going in my direction but he refused. He could only drop us off at the bus stop, and he did. We watched him drive off and his taillights disappear into the darkness. Melody checked the time on her phone, it was 3 a.m., and there was no sight of transport. We sat by the roadside waiting and praying, it was freezing cold; Jack Frost's kisses graced our cheeks, but the cold was the least of our worries. I was scared that we were going to be robbed or worse kidnapped. I kept praying that it would not happen. The street slowly came to life, people popping out of dark corners, some were homeless people heading out to start their day, and others were vendors coming to set up their stall. A woman set up her stall next to us, she had sweets, two huge pots she placed on a fire she made; one pot was half filled with oil she was going to make doughnuts and the other pot had maize she was planning to boil. We sat there as the night turned into gray and started to pick some color, an orange hue sneaked in from the east just a little bit as if it were shy to show off her splendor. At about 4:30 a.m. Melody found her lift home, and I still had to wait. Honeydew taxies only started to operate at 5:00 am or later, I was lucky that it came soon after Melody's taxi left and I got in. inside there were five men including the driver, I hadn't noticed until I found myself inside the taxi. My heart was pounding; I thought they were going to do something to me. The sun was barely up yet and I had to get home and

rest if I was going to be at the restaurant at 6 a.m. or latest 6.30 a.m...
The sounding alarm was a reminder that I did not get much sleep at all and I did not have a choice but to go to work.
Working at a club was much more frustrating than the restaurant and it was more depressing when we, Melody, and I were tasked to clean the new place before it opened. Located on the upscale land near Montecasino_ the place I never thought I would ever be near it. The place was once some kind of brothel, Gerry, who was assigned to 'guard' us while we washed the dishes and scrubbed the toilets, the filthy puke deserving toilets. We tried having fun while cleaning, but it was somewhat difficult considering the hours we cleaned without eating; especially the first day, we wished to be back at the restaurant where we could nibble on bits of vegetables we chopped. It was only after three days when we came across a pantry that was filled with nearly expired food. We managed to forage what we could and made coffee with the coffee maker that we had 'cleaned'. As I ate the funny tasting bread and cockroach-smelling coffee, my life flashed before my eyes. This was what my life had become after my father's death, he used to tell me that I would miss good food one day whenever I was fussy with whatever they had bought, I just did not expect it to happen like this. It was bad, but we ate it either way, we wanted to have something to keep us going and this was it. I missed home a lot while I was cleaning the soon to be new club; the heavy lifting took a toll on my chest that caused my asthma to flare up. I never complained there was no one I would complain to anyways. I just boiled water in my aunt's kitchen added a few drops of lemon and took a quarter of my salbutamol tablets which knocked me out after an episode of palpitations and uncontrollable jerking like a drug addict. I never complained, and I never said anything, whom would I tell?

There was one funny moment in the midst of this hardship. We were busy cleaning the rooms, Melody in rooms that looked like they were used as bedrooms_ we thought since it was once a brothel, and I was in the toilets. The men's toilet did not have a light bulb and the hallway was quite scary. I could hear Melody opening doors and fighting off spiders and roaches that maybe fell on her, she would scream so loud and I would laugh at her, happy that I did not have to deal with all that she was facing. My job was easy, I would pour in the toilet bowl cleaning liquid and scrub with the toilet brush and give the toilet bowl a flush and repeat the process but the second time leaving the disinfectant in and flush when we were about to leave. A hack we learnt with the other two toilets that were located in the restaurant wing. Melody screamed from the other room, this time her scream was more of a shriek and the light in the women's toilet was flickering, suddenly there was a flicker in the men's bathroom as well; it was strange because we knew that the bulb did not work. She screamed again, this time things fell over and I rushed to where the screams were coming from, I found her standing by the doorway staring inside. I went up to her and looked in the direction she was facing and I saw it too. Chains hooked onto the wall and blood splatters decorating the wallpaper.

"*I am not cleaning that!*" I said walking a few steps closer. I wanted to verify if it was really blood. Melody followed closely behind me, with her broom in hand.
"*What do you think it is mnawami*?" she had assumed the role of a big sister, considering

that she was older than me and her totem was the same as mine. *"I think it is blood,"* I replied moving a little closer. *"How do you think it got there? Moreover those chains; what kind of place is this?"* she asked again. I did not respond, at this time we were both at the centre of the room staring and trying to make sense of what we were seeing. Without warning the lights went out and a loud bang came from the bathroom, we shoved and pushed each other out of the room and flew out the hallway and into the kitchen then the lounge area and outside to the parking area. None of us said a thing, my heart was pounding in my breast, my knees were wobbly, and I could not catch my breath. I was certain that there was a ghost in the building; it was the only reason I could think of that made sense. It was the only reason that explained the blood splatter on the walls. The first thing that came to mind was that it was a tortured ghost, yes, definitely; why would they have chains hanging on the walls and the whips we found? I was certain that the club was more than just a brothel, I had heard a lot about South Africa, but being in a place where people had been tortured was the icing on the cake. Gerry came and found us sitting on the patio; he parked his red bakkie with a white canopy just in front of us.
"You girls are fast, did you finish already?" he asked as he approached us. We looked at each other as if we were debating on who was going to tell him first.
"*Gerry!"* Melody broke her silence, her voice was shaky, and she could barely breathe. I on the other hand was much calmer I jumped in.
"There is a ghost in the club." I stared blankly at Gerry, who in turn burst out in laughter. He walked into the restaurant side and we remained seated staring at him as he walked in.
"you are crazy, there is no ghost here" he called us back into the building. Reluctantly we rose to our feet and moved to the door. We peeked in as if we were expecting to see the ghost standing next to Gerry.
"If there is no ghost, why did the lights flicker?" Melody asked, I took a step further. I was still scared, but I had left my phone next to the coffee machine and I wanted it.
"*Probably a power outage, this place was a club guys*." With assurance in his voice, he tried to convince us to finish what we were doing.
"A club that tortures people? We saw the chains Gerry." Melody gained the courage to speak confidently.
"*Chains?"* he inquired.
"Yes, Melody and I saw a chain on the wall in one of the rooms." I said sitting on the sofa that was a few meters away from the door.
"*Oh those chains*." He giggled. "*Yes and a whip*" melody added. Gerry went to the host's table and pulled out a whip similar to the one we had seen.
"*You mean this?"* he whacked the table and went up to Melody.
"*Yes."* We both said in a chorus like manner.
"*Nah man! They used these in their brothel, you know the SNM. You surely knew that this place was once meant for that."* He explained the whip's use, but did not quite tell us what SNM meant. We told him that we did not want to clean because we were still distraught. We decided to pick up where we left off the next day and my pick up we meant picking up the cleaning equipment and cleaning elsewhere. We partially did not buy the SNM nonsense he was talking about_ well not until I googled it.

Chapter 18

I was now twenty-one, and still in the restaurants trying to earn a living. I stopped working at 1860, the pay was not sufficient and the conditions had become too painful. I owed my uncle money and I was failing to pay my school fees. School was out of the question anyway, I never had time for it; my new job demanded my whole self, I started early and knocked off very late and by the time I got home, I would be exhausted. Getting my third job was not that difficult; though it required me to be patient_ and patience is something I am not good at. That morning, I lied to the manager at the Indian restaurant I was working at, and faked a tummy ache just so that I could look for another job. I walked to a mall that was a few kilometers away from the new complex we were now staying at. I remember wishing for a quick way back home as I walked. When I arrived at Northgate mall, I took out my CVs from my handbag and entered the first restaurant that was just by the entrance. Ocean Basket was a seafood restaurant; the waiters wore blue T-shirts and blue jeans. I met a waiter standing by the doorway and he smiled at me as I walked towards him, he must have thought that I was a customer as the restaurant was dead quiet. Disappointed by my reason being at the restaurant he led me to the manager who was a short round man with a stub nose.
"Hello, my name is Elizabeth," I said as I tried to calm my nerves. I always get nervous upon meeting new people, but find ways to speak confidently.
"Hello Elizabeth, how can I help you?" he pulled a chair and leaned over it with the palm of his hands and smiled at me. *"I'm looking for a job as a waiter, here is my CV,"* I forced a smile as I handed him the four paged document.
"I see here it says you are Zimbabwean, do you have a permit to work here?" he paged through the document and looked at me. I thought about my fake permit, I thought if I told him that I didn't have one, I wouldn't get the job and if I told him that I had it, he might ask to see it and notice that it was fake. "*Yes, I do.*" I kept my sight fixated on him. "*Why are you leaving your current job?*" he asked and I told him that it was far from where I stayed. He took the CV and rolled it and rubbed his head with the palm of his hand, *"Sadly, we don't have any openings as you can see this place is quiet, I will keep your CV on file though.*" He said.

As his words fell on my ears, despair coursed through my body. I walked in and out the other restaurants and they told me the same thing the short manager had said. I walked to another mall located in Northriding; it was my last resort before I went home. I had only one CV left and one ounce of hope left. I avoided people that I came across, thinking that they were either tsotsis or worse kidnappers. Though there were times I wished to be kidnapped, as strange as it sounds I thought maybe if I disappeared from the face of the earth it would have made the world a better place. Most times, I wanted to be invisible, this was when I became more acquainted with the voices that used to keep me up. They became my friends; they gave me comfort when I needed it, they understood me. I came to a restaurant called Dros; I thought it was a coincidence as the restaurant that was next to the 1860 Indian restaurant I was running away from was also called Dros. It was eleven a.m. and the restaurant was also quiet, hunger was nibbling at my stomach and my feet were now fighting to break free from my shoes. I entered the restaurant and saw a skinny waiter who was about my height, I had heard him playfully scolding another waiter in Shona, and so I instantly used that language as my mode of communication. He was very helpful and very friendly; I learned that his name was Lucas. He gave me a seat and told me to wait for the manager. I sat in the booth that was by the entrance and waited, some waiters came and tried to make a conversation with me, and I just kept it short. Hours passed and the manager did not come, and each time I wanted to give up waiting the waiter stopped me from leaving. Finally, the manager came and Lucas told him that I was his little sister and was in need of a job, he asked for my CV and paged through. Lucas kept nagging Charlie the manager who then took the CV, rose to his feet, and told me to come for training on Thursday. I was stunned; I could not believe that I had finally found a job. I walked out feeling pleased with myself and thankful for Lucas who was a voice of reason that told me to wait.

Now I had a job and no transport money, walking was the only option on the table. It was a few kilometers away from the complex, a two or three hour walk to be precise. I recall one hot morning and I was sweating through my white t-shirt, the first time I walked to work, I was still a trainee then, my jeans were still sagging, and I was so flimsy you would have sworn that the wind was pushing me forward. I had my earphones plugged into my ears and my thoughts echoed behind my schizophrenic playlist, the only way to keep me sane.

Each day that I walked to work, I felt further away from the world. I could never tell anyone what was going on with me. I recall one customer, Brian, asked me about my commute to work. He was an old man, playful and I should say very kind for a white Afrikaans male especially towards black people. He stayed near at one of the complexes that were near the one I stayed at; he drove a pre-loved red Mazda 323 that was rather small for his giant stature. He saw me walking to work one day because I had my earphones plugged into my ears and focused on the long walk I did not see him drive past. When I arrived at work, I saw him sitting in the bar area while the other waiters were finding ways to start cleaning around him. He was a regular customer at Dros, so they never chased him away even if he came before shop was open.

"I always see you walking in the morning, why?" he said as he pulled me by the hand. I noticed that his right hand was missing a thumb. I smiled and tried to free my hand from his grip, before I could answer him he continued speaking, *"Are you a health freak? Trying to keep fit?"* he let go of my hand and ran his eyes from my head to toes. My sagging jeans came to mind and wondered how he would think that I was trying to be fit, could he not tell that I was just a frame housing a broken soul.

"Yes." I lied through my teeth, *"walking is healthy."* I smiled and left him standing next to the barrel that served as a table in the bar area. I did not know where I would start the story of my life. I did not know how to tell a stranger that I drowned my pillow with my tears at night and wore a smile to cover up my puffed eyes in the morning.

Crying was the only outlet that I had, besides puffed eyes and a splitting headache the next day it never gave me anything tangible. I had always been an emotional child, I understand I was grown and had to take care of my issues differently like how all grown-ups do, but it felt as though I was shoved into adulthood and I was not ready.
I 'fitted in' perfectly with my new family at Dros. I was a misfit puzzle but with all the right edges. I would stare at my reflection in the bathroom mirror and I would see a trapped little girl yearning to break free. In this mirror, I saw my true self. I saw a crooked smile, hiding a frown and holding up tears as best as it could. No one at the restaurant knew what I was going through, they had not earned the right to know my battles; I felt as if none of them were strong enough to help me. I breathed pins but I just could not throw in the towel, my mom did not raise a quitter.
I would walk out of the bathroom with a smile much perfect than the legendary Mona Lisa's. *Good morning, I'm Lizzie and I'm your waitress today, would you like to know our breakfast specials,* whenever I said those words I felt like adding and *please take me back home to Zimbabwe I'm trapped here.* I always kept my smile and continued with my work.

Sometimes I lurked in dark corners, behind the wall or banners and stare at families; somehow, I would zone out and see my family at the table, happy, laughing and having a great chat. On nights like these I would be reminded me of one night a few days or weeks before my father's passing; mom had prepared spaghetti and chicken stew. I guess a friend of my father's had paid him his dues for a work he had done or he had loaned him a few dollars; whatever it was, saw my parents splurging a little. I remember the three of us, seated in the living room, candles on the table_ because we did not have electricity, and I was gobbling down my plate of food. Somehow, I lifted my gaze toward my father who was staring at me as grazed down the food like a hungry traveler. He did not say anything, he just looked at me and smiled and then he scraped some spaghetti from his plate on to mine. I missed those moments, and seeing the little white girls with their fathers sent me to places in my mind I wished I could get back in real time.

Chapter 19

I held Peter Stuyvesant blue, the pack of ten in my hands tightly as I contemplated if I needed another smoke. The lights in the house were still on, so I stalled; I did not want the gory eyes of my 'new family' glaring piercingly at me. I hated the silence in the house; it screamed so much and always sent me to bed crying. I felt like a burden more and more. It made me wonder what wrong had I committed to deal with such emotions. Questioning them was not optional; they had let me stay with them for far too long an equivalent to a new lease on life after my father's departure. Though suffocating it might have become, no one ever complained aloud. I hated the comments that were passed, telling me to find blessers like other girls my age. I hated the remarks made, about other girls having kids and being married at my age. These made me feel unwanted. Probably no harm was meant when people said all that_ I was old enough to have both but it was a known fact that I was trying to put myself through school and my work took up the other half of my time, I had no time to be thinking about marriage. Those three words (*girls my age)* were like bee stings to my ears; life had suddenly turned into a race but one that I maintain my standards at the same level as the other girls. I could not be like them; I was different. Surely, it was my own insecurities and pressures placed on my head to be perfect_ I had to be perfect.

I started smoking because of my nosebleeds; they had become worse.
I became worried, thinking that maybe I had a terrible disease that was sneaking up on me. My spirit guide came to me in a dream and instructed that I breathe smoke out through my nose for three days. I found it weird, but the way my nose bled alarmed me. I took one of the cigarettes I had from the box I sold singles to smoking clients; I did just as I was instructed, after the third day the nosebleed stopped. I was astonished and happy. Then I was hooked, each time I smoked I felt a huge burden exiting with every exhale. Cigarette in hand I took one long pull, thoughts of how I came to be here hounded me. I felt as if the deep inhales I took gathered all my troubles and when I exhaled, they scampered away into the darkness. I would sit under the staircase, staring at the stars and thinking about how my life would have been if I had not come to South Africa. I was initially supposed to use a quill from a hedgehog, burn it and allow the smoke to go into my nose. I had no idea where I would get a hedgehog's spike, but the nosebleeds needed to be attended to in haste. This was when the cigarette option came in, not sure if this was made up in my head or my spirit guide gave me that option but I was supposed to do it once...

I do not remember choking on my first pull, I had learnt by looking at how the smokers at the restaurant did it and it must have come naturally, having a father who smoked nearly on a daily basis. I never had to hide them. They knew that I would sell loose cigarettes to customers to get extra cash; all the waiters at the restaurant did that.
I think my road to depression-vile started when we went to a party at a house that belonged to my uncle's friend, just a few weeks after my arrival. I was introduced to them

and the hosts led us to the living room where their kids were sitting. I sat with my cousin as I watched my uncle and his wife head to the table that was set outside. My cousin started playing with her friends and the adults were chatting away enjoying their alcohol. I sat by myself in the living room, looked out through the French door, and noticed how happy everyone seemed. Suddenly all went dark, memories of my mother flooded my mind; then it as if dawned on me that all the children at the party had both parents present and I did not. I felt a sharp pain going through my heart, I was miles away from my mother, and all of a sudden, I felt that I was an outsider. It felt like I did not belong, surely my uncle was there but I was not used to him. This was the first time I stayed with him and his family and it felt like I was just and extra person shoved into their lives.
I wanted to go back home, but at the same time I did not want to quit before I tried; I did not want to be a disappointment and besides my mother needed my help. I had promised my father before he died that I was going to look after my mother and make her proud.

It must have been when I watched my cousin with her father and it made me miss my own, everything felt hard to accomplish. When I left Zimbabwe for South Africa, I had hopes of continuing with school; I wanted to study something that had History, *I had always loved the past*. I always had a strong connection with the past.
A part of me knew that it might not happen, I did not have a father anymore who had hopes to see his little girl graduate, they were just empty hopes on my side. I have always felt like I needed some sort of validation for my existence. It was as if I had been handicapped and needed some kind of 'pat on the back' for the efforts that I took and when I did not get that, it took away a part of me. Slowly I felt myself deteriorating, and saw myself worthless. I wanted some kind of approval from my uncle, one that I would have gotten from my father if he were alive. Surely, it was pathetic of me to seek that kind of attention from him seeing that he was not my father, but he was the closest thing to a dad that I had. I kept a rulebook in my head that I followed, made sure that I did everything by the book; did not go out partying and always made sure I was home soon after work. I did not date, or hang around with boys just to make sure I did not create a bad record that could have me shipped back to Zimbabwe. I made sure that I was the picture of perfection, and hoped for someone to notice my efforts.

I was disillusioned in thinking that my uncle would be there for me just as my father would have been if he were alive. I thought everything would be 'normal'. This yearn to be seen by my uncle ate me up; it felt as though nothing I did mattered and my aunt's silent nature didn't help at all. I drowned myself with work and focused on being done with school just so that I could go back to where I felt I was seen. It seemed as though the more I tried to ignore the things that were happening around me the more I was sinking and drowning in my loneliness. You wonder how one gets lonely when surrounded by Family. At my uncle's home, it felt like there was a certain way I was supposed to behave and I was not doing it. This was the same even when I was at school. It was painful being a teenager; conversations with my school friends did not gel perfectly; they would converse about boys and parties while I did not have any juicy story to entertain them. I felt like an outsider amongst my school friends and I felt like an outsider amongst family.

I felt forced to be around people who did not understand who I was, and what I wanted from life and slowly I faded into the background.

I did not have much of a social life and being trapped in the food industry never gave me time to meet people. I was an introvert anyways or maybe I was turned into one, I do not know anymore but I preferred to be on my own and did not mind people not knowing me. Being a loner could have been part of me since before I came to South Africa. Here I was sitting under the stairs smoking a pack of cigarettes like a professional would do. I always felt forced into people's lives, I felt like I was the odd one out. They did not understand me, no one did. Most times, I preferred my own companionship to a bunch of family members that exuded a strong stench of stranger. This yearn to fit in sent me into a cold and dark hole, I would crawl into whenever I was alone and find myself in my own world and when I was around people I would put on an act like everything was great when it was actually topsy turvy. I did not have trouble at work because everyone was there doing their own thing and no one expected anyone to act in any way.
Now that I was a professional smoker, I let my troubles float away with the smoke. I knew how to pull on the cigarette long enough not to choke and could alternate the exhales between my mouth and nose. I would do this under the watchful eye of the moon, as if I was communicating with spirits who knew answers to all the problems I had; yet some questions remained unanswered, still I savored the moments I had with the smoke. I used to feel as if smoking brought me closer to my father; I missed him more when I was in South Africa than when I was still back home. He used to smoke too and said it calmed his nerves, now I could relate to this. I wanted to escape the prison I was in and smoking somewhat made it feel like I was half way to who knows where. Confiding in my mother was part of my self-therapy routine that involved walking and listening to music; on a lengthy call, I would tell her everything that took up much of my mind, she knew about the things that made me happy and the things that made me sad. I feel like when I moved from the Indian restaurant to Dros, I became more depressed. It was as if I was being sucked in deeper into a vortex of misery and emotional torture.
When the lights in the house went out, I would quietly enter and head straight into the bathroom. There I would shed all my tears while warm water trickled on me from the showerhead. It was therapeutic, calmed the nerves that were left behind when the others escaped with the smoke. After I was done with the shower, I would tiptoe into my cousin's bedroom and grab my pills. These were meant for my allergies, but I found them perfect for getting me to sleep. I would take a couple and stare into the darkness waiting for them to kick in. They made me forget where I was and numbed the pain that I was feeling. The pills became part of a routine that kept me sane.

I told my mother everything; except about me being hooked on to the smokes and the failed suicide. It seemed as though none of my escape options where working and I was feeling beyond suffocated. One night, after a gruesome shift at work, I was slowly considering quitting school, because I did not have time for it anymore and the debt was way over my head, everything seemed to be working overtime against me. I felt like I was a million miles away from home and it was starting to feel like I was never going to go back home. I felt trapped and without my smokes, I was lonely again; I had suddenly decided to quit. A decision I was yet to find out that I took it in haste; one of my best qualities, being an impulsive decision maker. I threw the packet that had about ten cigarettes left from the pack of twenty I had bought in a miniature river that flowed from the park reaching the main road. I remember watching the pack floating along the river and the lighter slowly sink. I wanted to dive into the water and take back what I had lost, but I did not know how deep the river was. Later that night, I sat on the carpeted floor in my cousin's room, took out my allergy tablets; I had about five or six remaining in the pack, I laid them in front of me and thought how peaceful it would be if I slipped a couple more in my mouth and just sleep for good. The pressure had gotten to me the silence tormented me; my cousin was fast asleep as well as everyone else in the house. I felt hopeless I did not need a suicide note, everything was in my diary, and my mother knew every detail.

Tears flooding my eyes, I popped one pill and looked at the little instruction; LEADS TO DROWSINESS, TAKE ONE TO TWO TABLETS, suddenly my eyes shifted to the bottom where other indications screamed what I wanted; MAY CAUSE HEART PALPITATIONS... I paused at that word, my mind wandered off. I thought about my mother, figured she would start a new life without me in the picture, one without stresses and insults being hurled at her. I was ready to go. I texted my mother told her how much I loved her and swallowed the remaining pills. Nothing else mattered at that moment except for my escape, I slithered into the blankets, beside my cousin; she was in a deep sleep she did not even move. I closed my eyes, said a prayer and a huge blanket like wave came over me and I felt my body relax.

Suddenly, I heard a faint ringing noise that gradually increased. I heard ducks quacking; and the alarm grew restless and yelled louder than usual. I opened my eyes and saw my cousin struggling with the noise; as always she had set the alarm much earlier than the time she was supposed to wake up, a prank that was getting boring. I woke up fumbling for her phone on her side table; the longer I took finding the phone the louder the rowdy alarm screamed. My aunt and uncle yelled from their room, as I continued to look for the noisy gadget and finally found it under the sofa. As I went through the phone changing the settings, it became apparent there were no palpitations after all. I felt robbed; I did not understand why I could not escape.

I wanted to end my life because I found it worthless; I had lost everything I ever cared for and the feeling of being a burden was no help at all. I was tired, not of living but of not being seen. I yearned to be seen and acknowledged of the person I was and becoming, it felt as though no one noticed my efforts and it was choking me. I did not consider the hurt that I could have been causing my mother, I was selfish yes, but was doing something for my selfish reasons a good thing? It would have done some good, I would not burden people with my presence, and they would just move on. Surely not my mother, it would have taken her time but I was aching and I could not fake a smile while my pillow drowned in my tears each night. I went to work later that morning, a bit bummed that I could not leave the hole I was in; I kept this embarrassing incident to myself. I was a failure, I failed to finish school, and I failed at everything else in life. I could not understand why I was a misfit in life and one in death; it seemed as though even death did not want me. Had I become so repulsive that even the underworld did not deem me fit to grace it with my presence? My shift dragged along as I questioned my purpose for existence.

Chapter 20

That morning I did not feel like working, I was too sad to fake a smile and play happy server, so I went upstairs with my phone and earphones in my apron pouch. Making sure that no one saw me I slithered on to the corner booth, which was well hidden from the security cameras. I plugged my earphones into my ears and started to play my music, I skipped through my schizophrenic playlist, as none of the songs made me feel any better. I plotted my escape again; dying had proved to be a foiled plan so I wanted to run away. I thought if I could just jump into a stranger's car after my shift and end up God knows where my stresses might melt away. It seemed too easy, a part of my conscious thought I would not get far enough before something terrible happened to me. That was not an issue, I wanted to kill myself and it was a complete fail; someone else doing it was bonus. I wanted to get out more than anything else.
I thought of a friend of mine who was working in Cape Town, game drive or something. He invited me there, a casual visit. I thought would take up his offer. Go to Cape Town and disappear somewhere on Table Mountain, I was going to leave without anyone knowing. Probably tell my mother save her the heartache, I would ask her not to tell my uncles. I would go without a trace, never come back to Johannesburg. That was the plan; *they* would not miss me. I thought.
I did not go through with it. I was just too coward I guess, no wonder I failed on the suicide.

I connected my phone to the restaurant Wi-Fi and went on YouTube, I started to stream through funny videos and music parodies; I wanted something to get my mind off the failed suicide. I was starting to wonder how I was going to tell my mother about it, it was surely going to hurt her and I realized that I was very much inconsiderate in my actions. I did not even consider my cousin whom I was sharing a bed with she could have been traumatized; my actions could have hurt many people. I started to feel my eyes well up, it stung as if I had been sprayed by a pepper spray; I was horrible to think that the world revolved around me. Suddenly the playlist on YouTube changed to a meditation audio, I saw uploads of different meditation audios and videos. I thought to have a look at it and within a second, I was hooked, and slowly I zoned out.

I saw myself in a green garden, the air was clean and smelt like fresh lavender blossoms, and it just felt welcoming. It felt like home, like a place I had been before and for that moment, I felt happiness surge throughout my body; I was happy. Butterflies fluttered about and I could hear water trickling down, hitting the rocks and splashing gently at the bottom. I felt the grass hugging my feet, and the dew cooling them down. It all felt serene, I did not know where I was but I could not care less; I was out of the horrid place, one that felt like hell nothing but a cold hell. Suddenly I had a tap on my shoulder, which jolted me up from my nap. Confused and scared I jumped up from the seat and stumbled down the stairs. My friends who were sitting near the bottom of the stair broke out in laughter, just as I locked eyes with them.

"*What's wrong Liz, Did you see a ghost?"* they tried to keep a straight face only to burst out in laughter. As I was trying to catch my breath, I thought that they were mocking me; I had shared with them my experiences with the gift.

"I thought I felt someone tap my shoulder," I said to them confusion stirring in my head. I wanted to think that one of them might have passed through and tapped me, but that would have been impossible as the other entrance was locked, *I had locked it personally*. They could not have used the delivery entrance, no one did it was a death trap; most of the steps on the stairs had fallen out. Only a nut job would risk their life just to give me a scare. The only option was the main staircase, the entrance that led down into the restaurant, but I would have caught them before they could catch their breath. The flight of stairs on that side had about fifteen stairs if not twenty, *I think* and they were steep. One of my friends, who had been working at the restaurant longer than the three of us, pulled me to the side of the stairs while the other two remained standing at the bottom of the stairs, next to a table.

"*Did you say someone tapped your shoulder?"* He inquired. He had a worried look on his face when he asked me the question.

"*Yes, it was a gentle tap but it scared me."* His face went pale. At this moment, the other two had already left for their tables and I was getting worried.

"I heard that there was a ghost in this place, in fact I am sure that it once tugged my legs while I was taking a nap." I looked at him, shook. There was no way he was lying to me as his face showed more than fear. After telling me this, he left for his tables, and left me wondering if it could have been true that I had an encounter with a ghost. I considered other possibilities before settling with the ghost story like that someone could have tapped me and that same someone could have tugged Lucas during his nap. There was a manager, who liked pulling pranks; I walked up to him and tried to read his facial expression. I had hopes that he could have had something to do with it, but he was not quick on his feet; we could have seen him. Until this day, it remains a mystery, I never found out who tapped me and, I prefer not to know.

Chapter 21

The most confusing moments must have been when I met Marcy; I was on my way home from the hairdresser in Cosmo City, dressed in my navy blue and white striped skirt and gray tank top, my red sandals matched my new hair-do. I was tired of the usual black hair so I decided to put a different color. I felt girly, in my new weave and skirt; something I rarely did. I always went for the easy look, braids, jeans and closed comfortable shoes. I sat in the back seat of the Venture that was the regular transport from Cosmo to Northgate Mall. She sat in the front seat, busy punching her phone. The driver took a different route that I was not familiar with and I feared that he could get me lost.
"*Sorry Driver, I am going to Northgate Mall,*" I politely reminded him masking my fear of being kidnapped or worse.
"*Yes Sisi, I know.*" The driver responded. Marcy turned her head and looked at me.
"*Don't worry I am going to the same place I will show you where it is.*" She said and quickly glanced back to her phone. The car scurried away and I could see the top of the Coca-Cola Dome. My heart finally settled in its place and I prepared myself to get out of the car.
"*Wait for me!*" she said as she gathered her belongings. She was wearing khaki cargo pants, paired with timberland shoes and a brown almost army green T-shirt and a khaki sleeveless jacket. I waited, thinking about what I would say to a stranger.
"*Where do you want to go?*" she asked as we made our way through the entrance.

"*Pick N Pay, and then the taxis home,*" I responded and glanced at my phone. "*Cool, I will show you where it is. I'm Marcy*" she introduced herself and so did I. she seemed like a friendly person and her accent sounded like a South African native. She took me to the shop that I wanted to go to and after I had gotten what I had come to buy.
"*I want to catch a burger; if you are not in a hurry, please may you join me*?" I was a bit uncomfortable with accepting food from a stranger, but I also did not want to go home early that day. I thought what harm would befall me when I was with another female.
"*I'm not hungry.*" I said looking at the time on my phone.
"*Okay then, I will get you ice cream and a burger for me.*" she insisted. I did not want to seem rude and I had some money with me so paying for my own ice cream was not going to be an issue. We approached a KFC outlet that was just a few shops after the PnP store. We took a table and she went to the counter and placed the orders. As she ordered the food, I looked at her and started to wonder if she was one of the people, I had seen during the time I worked at Montecasino. She dressed like them and walked like them, I did not want to seem prejudicial, I was certainly not, but it boggled my mind and I wanted to know. We started talking and I found out that she was a photographer, I admired her work, and then she started complimenting Zimbabwean women. The way she described how we looked, questions flew into my head. It was so masculine and I was certain that she was definitely lesbian. Then she completely changed the topic and spoke about girly

stuff, at this point I was completely confused. I was now convinced that she was not, the whole time I sat with her I had a yes-no battle in my head. The fact that she could have been lesbian was no trouble with me at all, I just wanted to know if she was but I could not ask her.

We sat, talked, and laughed as if we were old friends. When it was time for me to go she showed me the way to the taxis I was supposed to take, we exchanged numbers and I watched her walk away as I continued to question her sexuality. Then she texted me asking if I had reached home safely, it felt a bit off but I responded to the text either way. Then the answer to the questions that were bugging me the whole day came in black and white. *I had a great day today, thank you for that. Do you believe in Soul mates?* I took a while to respond to her message. I was not sure where she was driving at with her question. I brought myself to respond, seeing that I was curious and it was eating me up.

Yes. I responded. *Well I think that today I have found mine.* She sent a smiley face after her text. I quickly responded with a congratulatory message. I have no idea why I said it in that manner but it seemed right.

You are the one I'm talking about. She said and I paused. I did not know what to say. The answer to my question was right in front of my eyes and I could not handle it. I told her that I was not lesbian and she responded saying she would teach me and I did not have to be one to fall in love. It felt uncomfortable to have a girl hitting on me. Carefully turning her down, I tried not to sound judgmental or against her beliefs, just like my previous boss used to tell me, *tell them to fuck off, but in a nice way*, I did that as gently as I could, not stepping on any toes.

When I told my mother about the incident she laughed at me, asked, *"What were you wearing?"*, and continued to laugh. I remained friends with Marcy, which was something important to me; offending people was never my cup of tea.

It must have been the red hair's fault and not my dress.

Chapter 22

She sat on table eight, the most uncomfortable seat anyone could ever ask for. Her eyes were peppery red, her nose swollen and her cheeks puffed up. She pulled out her phone, probably stared at the time or a message notification, and smashed the phone on the table face down. She wiped her nose with the back of her hand and I mastered the courage to talk to her. I did know how she was going to react towards me. She forced a smile as I introduced myself to her and asked her if wanted something to drink. I had now become good at waitering; it was more like second nature to me.
"Hie dear, tell me what the strongest whiskey on your bar counter is?" she sniffled; her voice was shaky as she spoke to me. I could tell that she had been crying for a long period.
"We have Johnny Walker Black," I responded with a smile trying to avoid showing the confusion that was buzzing in my head. As I spoke to her, I could feel my phone vibrating. The restaurant was too busy for me to attend to any calls so I let it ring.
"Gimme a double... no, make it two doubles in one glass of Johnny Black and a bottle of Merlot and one glass please... but first the whiskey." I left the menu on the table and left for the waiter's station with the extra cutlery. I punched in the order and instructed the bartender to pour the four shots of whiskey in one glass and I began to stress about the bottle of wine that I had ordered. I was not skilled at opening wines that had corks on; I was scared that the one I had ordered was one of them. I rushed to the kitchen looking for another waiter who had borrowed my corkscrew.

I returned to the bar with my corkscrew in hand, I felt my phone vibrate again as I was about to pull it out I glanced at my customer. She was cracking her knuckles and her wiping tears simultaneously; I suddenly remembered that amid my confusion I forgot to ask her if she wanted her whiskey on the rocks or neat. I quickly dashed to the kitchen to get a glass filled with ice, fast enough for my boss not to see or I would have been fired on the spot. My phone stopped vibrating for a little while, then again. I took the woman's order to her table and as I placed the glasses on the table, she grabbed the whiskey glass and gulped down the golden liquid and wailed some more. I felt an urge to ask her what was bothering her, as I could not put my finger on what could possibly make her sad. She was too pretty and definitely looked affluent to be troubled. My phone vibrated again, this time it really annoyed me. I placed my hand on top of my apron on the left hand side, in my jean pocket where my phone was.
"Can I have a single shot of your best vodka and a glass of ice cold water, please?" She pulled the bottle of wine to her and started to read the label.

Ignoring my phone, I rushed to the station and placed the order. My boss peered over my shoulder and noticed the drinks on my open table.
"Make sure you get some food orders through hey Lizzy, you haven't served a single plate of food today." He walked away.

I could not believe that he was saying I had not served any food, this was my fifth table since the morning, and the traffic had only just begun. My phone vibrated again, I started to be worried; I was thinking that it could have been my mother calling or worse someone calling because something had happened to my mother. I took the vodka order to her table, she had already opened the wine bottle_ it was a screw top so she did not need a corkscrew. I saw a tear escaping into her wine glass; I too made my escape into the bathroom. I had to check my phone, as I unlocked it I looked at the time it was only seven pm. I then noticed the number of missed calls that I had received, all fifteen of them came from my uncle's number. Immediately I called him back, my heart was pounding, what ifs started flying through my head. I put the toilet seat cover down, sat on the toilet, and bit my nails on my left hand as I waited for my uncle to answer.

I suddenly felt tears flooding my face; I stared at my phone's screen as I hung up the call. Someone walked into the bathroom; I wiped my tears and gathered myself. I pretended as if I was checking if the toilet paper had not run out. I walked out of the restroom as if I had seen that ghost that tapped my shoulder. I slid my phone into my pocket and went to table eight.
"*Ma'am, are you ready to order something to eat*?" I forced a smile as I asked. Her bottle of merlot was halfway through, so was her bottle of water. I pulled the empty glasses towards one end of the table and tried to make eye contact with my customer. Her big beautiful brown eyes were dilated and tears slowly oozed out of them like honey from a beehive, I felt mine rushing as well, so I held my head back and exhaled almost quietly.
"*Bring me another whiskey but this time a single shot and put lots of ice.*" She paused for a moment staring at me. I noticed that she had seen something; I put my right hand on my cheeks to feel for tears and quickly grabbed the glasses.
"*You can take the menu; I don't think I want to eat anything for now*." She said pushing the menu towards me. I had not brought a tray so I left the menu behind as I went to ring up the order.

I found her pouring more wine into her glass and I placed the whiskey in front of her. *"I hope you are not driving tonight ma'am?"* I inquired as I was getting worried about the amount of alcohol she had taken in; I did not want to be responsible for an accident.
"*Never trust men sweetie...*" She pulled my hand and caressed it her hands they were soft and warm. *"... They promise you the world, give you the wedding of your dreams and when you face a trouble like mine, they call you names."*
She emptied the bottle into her glass, took a small sip, and continued; I wondered why she was telling me whatever she was telling. I had asked her about how she was going to get home and she completely shifted to something else.
"*He calls me a witch because I cannot bear him children, he said I wasn't woman enough...*" she started crying. *"...So I drink, to make up for what I lack,"* she took a big sip of the wine and placed the glass precariously on the table. I positioned the glass properly on the table and tried to comfort her the way I know how to. I had never been in her situation; I did not know what to say to her. I knew drowning your sorrow in alcohol was never the answer neither was smoking but sometimes situations and problems in life push you to do things you never imagined yourself doing. You just become trapped into it.

She looked at me and sat properly in her chair. *"Look at me dumping my troubles on you, when you seem to be facing a whole lot of issues,"* I tried to smile instead my eyes became watery; I remembered the short conversation I had, had with my uncle.
"I can tell that there is a lot bothering you Hun, this is not your body... I mean you don't look like someone who is happy, you have lost a lot of weight." My watery eyes started to flow, I wanted to tell her everything, but I did not know where to start. Moreover, she was a stranger; I was not good with opening up to strangers. How was I going to tell her that I could no longer pay for my fees because I was knee deep in debt and I could not get help? How was I going to tell her that I did not fit in with people who were supposed to be family? How was I going to tell her about the call I received? I felt worthless, I could not figure out my purpose on the planet. Not that I ever complained I was trying to find my feet and pull myself together. I felt like my efforts were not seen. Each gulp she took told a story, it told both our stories. I ran to cigarettes and she to wine, in our differences we were the same. I guess like me, she thought that the bitter whiskey and vodka would bring her the salvation she desired.

After that day, that woman stopped coming to the restaurant, and during that time, I constantly beat myself up for not taking her number. I felt like I owed her, as if I was supposed to help her and I could not or more like I did not help her. I felt guilty for giving her the alcohol.
Days passed and each one had me thinking about her, especially on this particular day; another woman walked in, she ordered a whiskey similar to the previous woman's order. As I went to get her order, one of the waiters called out to me while I was rushing to the kitchen to check on a different order. *"Hey Liz! Your customer is crying; what did you do to her*?" I took the double shot of Johnny Walker black, neat, walked as fast as I could to the table, *she too sat on table eight* and found her wiping tears with tissues. I asked her what the matter was and she looked at me and smiled.
"I'm fine Hun, how much do I owe you? I need to get back home, my son almost died, I found him floating in the pool. I'm still shaking but I needed a drink away from home." she sniffled and took a sip from her glass. She seemed so calm for someone who almost lost her child. She fumbled for her purse then she realized that she did not have a purse neither did she have shoes on. She had frantically walked out of the house with her car keys and came to the restaurant. I wondered how she got the courage to leave her son after such a terrifying incident. The first instinct I had was to take the empty glass from her and advise her to go home to her child. It might have looked weird for someone who was half her age reprimanding and instructing her to return to her child, but was the only good thing I could do. I failed to help the other woman; I did not want another guilty conscious knocking on my brains. She left, with her senses still intact and I walked her out. I watched her getting into her car, and she drove off.

She came back the next day and asked for me, she wanted to settle her bill; I had already done it for her, but I was happy that she was okay and so was her son. I felt a surge of energy coursing through my veins, feeling like I had done well; though I was not, sure what good deed I had done. *I only served them alcohol.*

Chapter 23

I moved out of my uncle's house, my father's black leather bag in one hand and three black garbage disposable bags with my other items in the other hand; though not as exciting as it sounded. It is not that I wanted to continue staying with them despite how I felt, but I was not stable enough to start living on my own. It had been a topic raised a while back and was inevitable; it may have been a time for me to start finding my freedom_maybe myself.

I was nervous; it was the first time I was going to be staying on my own. It somehow felt like my first real step to freedom. My new home was a tiny square shaped one roomed apartment conjoined to another room that was similar in shape and in between the two was a rectangular shaped bathroom that had a tub, washing machine and a toilet bowl. My room had a chirped ceiling and wooden floor that was a breeze to clean. Close to the window, on the left was a fitted cupboard and on the right was my air pumped bed. It felt more like a prison than a house but I had no choice I hardly had any furniture so I had to endure the hollow room.

My new place was located in a foreigner-populated area of Cosmo City; one would think that I should have felt at home considering the number of Zimbabweans that lived in the area. I felt more lost, only when I was at home; I felt lonely, as if I had been cast out of society. I remember the day I moved in, the room was filthy and stuffy. The smell of dust filled the air and the floors seemed as if someone had poured sand from outside. There was a stained mattress hideously placed on the floor and next to it was an empty cupboard that could have been playing the role of a side table or mini-wardrobe; when I opened the drawers, it harbored a family of cockroaches. On the opposite side was a fitted cupboard that stood comfortably next to the window On the other side of the room was a dirty plastic table with wobbling legs. I flung open the windows, removed the soiled mattress, cupboard, and table, and started sweeping, thanks to my landlady who gave me the cleaning equipment. I mopped the whole place with the Domestos I found in the bathroom. After hours of grueling work I pumped my bed, I remember it looking like a real mattress after I had put the blankets on. I put my small bag in the small cupboard and the big suitcase underneath the plastic table. It gave the table support and I was able to use it for my laptop and other small things. After everything was put in place, I needed something to cover the window, as I did not have a curtain; I used one of my bed covers as the curtain.

I didn't have any pots or pans neither did I have a stove, I remember feeling hungry and dashing to a tuck shop I had seen on my way to my new place. I bought a bread meal that contained potato chips, Russian sausage, and polony topped with tomato sauce; they called it a Kota because of the size of the bread that was used. Lucky for me I had some change left from paying rent. Around suppertime, I sat in my four by four room with a movie playing on my laptop. I ate my food staring at the tiny screen of my laptop. The echo in the room made me feel as lonely as a hermit, thoughts flooded my head; I was scared of being by myself. The cracking noises outside seemed as if they were coming for me, even though my door was locked I did not feel safe. The cold was nibbling at my cheeks and I knew that winter was fast approaching and I did not have that many blankets. I had only bought comforters; I rarely had time for sleep and I never thought that I would need blankets because of my job. It was foolish of me, and I do not have any logical explanation for my stupidity. I depended on my electric blanket, and placing a bunch of clothes at the base of my pump bed and using the few blankets I had to cover myself. I unknowingly plugged my electric blanket throughout the night and I would wake up drained. I did this half way through winter explaining my mysterious lack of energy whenever I woke up.

My landlord was a young woman probably in her mid-30s, with an average height and a dark caramel toned skin. Sindi was a Zimbabwean based in South Africa; she spoke Ndebele and Zulu fluently and would try to speak to me in Shona though her accent was as terrible as when I tried to speak in Xhosa. She had been staying there for a much longer period than I had and had established for herself a business. Her tuck-shop was located about a kilometer from the house; there she sold everything from candy, groceries, and other necessities, I later found out that she sold beer secretly as well.

My new 'Off Day' routine, since I started to stay on my own was pretty simple; laundry, eat some Ace instant porridge and movies.
Ace instant porridge, the only food I had, that and a bottle of concentrated orange juice or *was it mango juice*? I could not afford to splurge on groceries to have home cooked meals; I had to save money for rent, and I did not have a stove neither did I have pots. I would pour the powdered porridge in a bowl that I had bought at Checkers, and head outside by the sink turn the faucet on and wait for the water to heat up as it came out. Yep! I used geyser water; Straight from the tap.
I ate the porridge every day for the first month, I had moved out of my uncle's house, three times a day when I was off work and once when I was working. While at work, I would forage for whatever the kitchen had and I could snatch without the managers looking or my friends would buy lunch then I would have my second meal of the day. Lucas was the one who used to get us lunch at his expense; him, and Tina.

My discovery of my landlady's secret business venture came with tiny heart attacks, as I had to deal with a police raid. I had finished washing my work uniform and made myself a bowl of Ace instant porridge and decided to watch a movie I had downloaded using the WIFI at work. I remember feeling unusually tired that day and I instantly dosed off while watching the movie. I woke up moments later and the movie was over, I thought to get some air; I took my bowl outside to the sink, as I was busy washing it and struggling with the porridge remains that had dried and stuck on to the bowl, I heard a police radio sounding from behind me followed by a siren. I turned my head to check what was going on and I saw a two police jeep and out came out officers, in my fright, I managed to count them up to ten as they jumped out of the vehicles towards me.

One black policewoman greeted me in a Zulu accent, I responded, at this moment my heart was pounding in my breast, and I felt weak in the knees. Another police officer this time a colored man asked me to open the screen gate in Afrikaans, I have no idea how I understood him as I was not good at speaking or comprehending Afrikaans. "*The keys are in my room,"* I quivered, a different black policewoman instructed me to go and get them in what sounded like Pedi. I knew this language because I had a Pedi friend for a while who taught me the basics and luckily for me "go" was one of the basics. I reached for the screen gate's keys that were plugged in the door keyhole and suddenly I started thinking about my passport. It was at an instant I could not remember where I had put it. While I was unlocking the screen gate the white police man placed his hand on the gate as if he wanted to push it open,
"*Who are you?"* he questioned in a stern voice.
My heart jumped, and in my mind, I traced the whereabouts of the passport. I wondered if it was in my workbag, then I remembered I had removed it because the bag was washed and hanging on the washing line.
"*I'm Elizabeth, and I'm a tenant here,"* I have no idea why I told them that I was renting the room because they had not asked me that question.
"*We are looking for Sindi, whose room is that?"* the colored policeman asked pointing at Sindi's door. Her room was adjacent to mine and in between us was the bathroom that served as a toilet and laundry room and next to my door was the sink.
"It is her room, but she is at work right now," I responded at the same time questioning my brain about the location of my passport.

At this moment my brain was betraying me, I could slowly hear it shutting down. "*Who did you say you are?"* the second white policeman questioned, jolting me up from the trance I was falling into. As I was about to respond to his question, another police woman shouted another question while peeking through Sindi's window, this time I could not respond to her as she spoke in what sounded like Sotho and I was still trying to respond to the other officer. With my brain not giving me any update on my passport, my body exposed my fear. I could feel every limb shaking as if they had suddenly disconnected from whatever they are supposed to be connected to. At this moment, I realized that I had to keep focused on my answers I had given at first.
"*I am only a tenant here, my landlady Sindi is not here she left for work in the morning.*" I confidently told them.
"*Where does she work?"* one officer asked, pulling out a tiny notebook and a pen.
"*I'm new in this area, but she owns a tuck-shop*," I said trying to peek at what she was writing; I saw my name in the notebook and instantly my mind went back to looking for my passport.
"*Does she sell alcohol, we want to search her room open it*!" another officer who was dressed in what looked like S.W.A.T uniform, it looked different from the other six officers.
"*I do not have the key to her room, and I do not know if she sells any alcohol. I am rarely here, so I rarely see her*." I added another explanation to what was supposed to be clear and straightforward answer session.

"*Where do you work?*" the officer with the note pad questioned staring dead into my eyes. "*I work at Dros restaurant in Northriding,*" she penned it down, and I continued to think about my passport, this time I was certain that I had lost it. While thinking about my passport I remembered that it had a fake permit still plastered on it, I felt sweat dripping under my T-shirt; I thought they could see how scared I was.
They started talking amongst themselves, and then one of the colored officers looked at me and asked if I knew what time, she was going to be back.

Scared that they might take me in for having a passport that showed I had returned to Zimbabwe and had a fake permit, I was an illegal citizen in South Africa. I turned to one of them with my chest heaved up collecting all the bravery within me and said,
"*I'm not sure, like I said I'm never home. You could ask the people who have been staying here longer than I have.*" I pointed at the main house that was in front of our cottage. They took down what I said in a notepad and they left. As I watched them leaving I felt a huge rush through my bones and my knees felt as if there was melting jelly in them. I went into my room, forgetting the bowl I was washing in the sink. I looked at my coat that was hanging on the wall and immediately remembered that my passport had always been in the left hand side pocket.

Chapter 24

The spiritual message I got about my grandmother's sister before the actual phone call came through bothered me, even though months had passed when it happened. I was certain there was a voice I heard telling me of the impending grief, but did not know who that voice belonged to. I replayed the past readings that I got from the prophets, they had claimed that I had a gift and one did mention that when it was the right time it was going to reveal itself to me. I started to wonder if that was the gift, they were talking about. It was not the first time that I heard voices so it did not scare me; I was curious to find out what type of gift it was. I thought, maybe I was destined to foretell on future events.

I started researching on the events that were taking place. I was surprised that a large number of people were going through the same things that I was facing. At one point, I thought that I was going crazy; I thought that the stress was getting to my head and I was creating things in my head. I recall this one day I was on my way to work, a taxi pulled up at the bus stop. I was about to board the taxi when I heard someone whispering into my ear, *do not enter that taxi.* I wanted to ignore the warning, but the push was stronger than my stubbornness. *The car is not safe; do not go in*, the voice said. Confused and heart pounding, I apologized to the driver and made an excuse that I had left my taxi fare behind, *"should I wait for you sisi?"* he shouted from the driver's seat. "*No it's fine; I will catch the next one, thank you.*" I smiled as I closed the door, and he drove away. I watched as the dust trailed behind the taxi creating a brown cloud in the air. Almost immediately, another taxi came, this time I asked, under my breath of course, *should I board this one*? almost immediately the voice replied, *yes.* I had no time to question if it certain because I was running late. I sat in the taxi with my earphones plugged into my ears. Even though music was playing, I was listening for the voice. The white van scurried away along the pot holed dusty road I saw the previous taxi parked on the side of the road. The passengers of that taxi were standing outside the car and the driver was waiving down the taxi I was in; I pulled out my earphones and tried to listen in on the two drivers' conversations. I heard the two talking about an accident that almost occurred. I looked outside the window in the direction of the first taxi; it lost its front wheel and was pure luck that they did not topple over.

I was dumbfounded and confused that day. I wondered what would have happened if I had ignored the message, maybe the accident could have been worse. The voice continued to make its presence known. I was torn between the thought of it being either an evil voice or a good one; I would pray each time I heard the voice speak to me and every time it did not leave. It would give me warnings on decisions that I had to make and get me out of trouble at the right time. I had to be certain that I was not going crazy, but did not have money to go to a doctor, or a shrink who was better suited for this aliment so I googled the 'symptoms' it was surprising knowing that this experience I was going through had a name. They called it Clairaudience; apparently, I was experiencing an enlightenment of the consciousness. Reading and knowing more about this weird experience made me more curious and brew a tiny bit of excitement. I found ways to control it from the other people in groups that were experiencing the same thing.

The gift matured, not too sure if I needed something else bugging my head, but it was quite the distraction that saved me from whatever that was going on with me. The more I learnt and meditated the stronger it became, to the point that I started experiencing premonitions. Playfully I would guess the customer's orders before they place them and would know when the boss was on his way. Then I met Alex, on one of the quietest Tuesday mornings the restaurant had ever seen. Grey clouds hovered and the cold nibbled on my fingertips; I was in no mood for work, *none of the waiters was in the mood that day,* moreover the customers that came in, ordered pots of tea and bottomless coffees. The smoking section had three miserable customers watching sports highlights and ridding off the previous night's hangover, the waiters were scattered about in the restaurant trying to find something to keep them busy; I was one of them, hiding from two elderly women who kept asking me to heat up their tea they had ordered since we had opened.

I sat on a bar stool staring outside through the huge window from upstairs. It was another of my escapes. The silence that came from upstairs encouraged my Clairaudient gift. A part of me enjoyed the fact that the messages I was getting were clearer but another part was terrified, I did not fully trust what was being whispered into my ear. While I was staring blankly out the window, I saw a small white car pulling up the restaurant complex driveway. My instincts urged me to dash downstairs, I found four waiters standing by the entrance and without hesitation, I told them that the car driving in was my client and I had already placed his drink order. One of the waiters, Nkosi who I think was skeptical about what I had told them inquired about the drink, suddenly I heard a whisper *"Stella,"* and without second-guessing, I told him what the voice had told me. He still had his doubts; I knew that if I did not grab the chance to serve the one person who did not look like a coffee drinker I was going to spend the rest of my shift bored upstairs. It was hard getting tables at Dros, especially if you were slow. They had a system in place, created by the waiters; "calling tables" was the only way one could get customers to serve. It involved a waiter standing by the entrance and screaming out the color of the car and race of the people who drove in or walked up to the restaurant, keeping in mind that the boss did not hear you and most importantly the customers. I had gotten the hand of the tactics, and perfected mine by finding a spot where I could see the clients before the other waiters could. My tactic worked, I got a client on one of the worst days of the week.

I waited patiently for the person to park his car, as he walked in I put on my biggest smile and led him to a seat in the bar area. As I was walking him to his seat, Nkosi wanted to snatch him away from me and I immediately told the customer that I had already placed his drink order and he seemed pleased at the quick service I had showed him. With a puzzled smile, he quietly sat across the huge flat screen that was showing a repeat of the previous night's rugby match. I went to the computer and punched in the order, praying

that I was right. I took the beer to his table and found him moved to another sitting area that was more secluded. I smiled as I took the beer to him, he looked at me, and the first thing I noticed was his blue eyes; they had a tinge of grey and they glimmered reflecting the restaurant lights.
"*How did you know that I drink Stella Artois*?" he questioned as he took a sip of his golden frothy beer. "*It was a wild guess,"* I gave half a laugh and introduced myself. He did not want a menu so I let him be with his drink. When he had about two or three glasses of the Stella draught, he asked if he could switch to the bottle and move to the smoking section. I helped him carry his glass and beer to a table at the end of the restaurant where one man was sitting drinking alone. The day suddenly started to move fast, I had myself three more tables that kept me busy with food orders. I went back to my blue-eyed customer, constantly checking on him even though he was now taking his sips at a slower pace and had joined the loner whom he had found seated in the smoking section. He decided to open a new table with his newfound friend; it disappointed me as it meant that I had to give the table to another waiter who was serving this other man before. My blue-eyed customer saw that I was saddened by the sudden switch; he kept his tab open just to keep me happy. My other three tables had their meals and left, and I had remained with his table, I went to the table and he started a conversation with me, he was quite inquisitive about who I was and the reason why I had to come to South Africa. I was getting tired of the question as it was one of the questions I came across every day that and the one of my age.

We spoke and shared laughs and I would occasionally disappear from his table just so my bosses would not give me trouble. Realizing this he asked for my number with the pretext that he would call and inform me when he needed to make a booking or come in for a drink. I did not think too much of his request and I gave him my number. It was just a number after all. He later left and texted almost immediately and that is when I learnt that his name was Alex. The next day as I was chatting with him on the phone he went back to the "wild guess" and he would insist that there was something more toward that intuition. I did not want anyone knowing about my "gift" so I would just create a story about being a good guesser, a fantastic one at that. He then invited me out for coffee as "friends" as he would put it. I accepted his invite keeping in mind that it was just a harmless cup of coffee. I met Alex at a restaurant that was in Fourways mall, as we walked into the restaurant I could feel eyes ogling at us and the waiters murmured under their breath. I think it was because he was a Caucasian man with a black girl; I would like to think that they were admiring me but im sure they had pegged me to be one of those girls who dated white men for money. I tried to look unbothered, and walked straight to our table with my head held high.

He sat in the chair across me, and the waiter asked for our drink orders. He ordered a Coke and me a Fanta; Alex's azure eyes glimmered each time he smiled, he had brown hair that was trimmed at the sides and high at the top. He was average height but certainly taller than me. We started talking about my "wild guess," it seemed as if he was interested in knowing how I was able to know all that I knew.
"So? How did you know what I drank?" he asked as he sat back in his chair and placed his

left leg on his right lap.
"*It was a lucky guess, a wild one,*" I giggled and my eyes shifted to the entrance leading inside the restaurant and I saw the female waiters still standing and obviously gossiping about me. I could tell because they were giggling and increased in number each time they whispered.
"*That was not a guess,*" he smiled and took a gulp of his coke and called the waiter to bring him a hunter's dry cider.
"*Then what was it?*" I looked at him and saw his eyes sparkle. I took a sip of my Fanta through the straw and looked away into the distance.
"*You are gifted, like me.*" he leaned over, resting his elbows on the table. He told me of his clairaudient experiences and it was amazing how most of it was similar to mine. He explained to me about auras and I recalled seeing them while I was working at the Gourmet Garage in Montecasino; I would see colorful bright lights around my reflection in the mirror and when I was feeling depressed they would be dark and eerie. I could see the auras he spoke off on him; his were brighter and almost blinding, and his eyes sparkled, at first I thought they were reflecting his white t-shirt that reflected the sun. *But we were in the shade.*
"*I see someone with you, I saw her the other day as well,*" my eyes widened, and honestly, I was scared. I wondered who this person could be, if he had said he saw a male figure I would have thought that it was my father.
"*Someone? Who?*" I asked panic-stricken.
"*I don't know she is an older woman.*" He paused,
"*Don't worry you are safe, she is looking out for you.*" I started to think of all the older women who could be looking out for me, and only one name came to mind it was that of my grandmother.

Chapter 25

Being awakened came with its own set of issues, it didn't make the issue of fitting in disappear instead it made me afraid of letting people close to me as I feared that they would not like me. I did not understand what was happening to me and I thought that no one else would understand me as well. I trapped myself in my head and I felt safe there. Now meeting someone who was like me, someone like Alex gave me some sort of relief; I was convinced that I was not crazy. The more I tried to distance myself from people the more they wanted me close to them.

While I was at Dros I became acquainted with many people, it was expected for me to create bonds with the people that I served on a regular basis; like the two young women that came one Tuesday night. The other waiters refused to serve them and practically dumped them on me. The reason why they did not want to serve them was that they only ordered wine. I recall going up to their table with a smile knowing fully what they were going to order but I wanted to find out if I could get them to order more than just wine. The two women were super friendly; they were actually excited to have me serving them. I remember spending half the night at their table, talking and they were so taken in with my story being in South Africa. Being at their table was not a problem at all, because Tuesday was one of the quietest nights we could ever have. Jen was tall and had beautiful long blonde hair; her eyes were cat like with a grey color and a tinge of green. She was fascinated by sky diving and every time they came to the restaurant she tried to get Tracy and I to go with her. Tracy was her friend; she was not as tall as Jen and had short blonde hair. She had brown eyes and was the most active and bubbliest one of the duo.

Whenever they came, giggles filled the air and gave me a sense of unconditional love that came from them. It could have been that I was hungry for that feeling of being loved, but when I was around them I felt like I mattered and I was noticed and that was all I wanted. Some of the waiters did not like the way I bonded with the white clients, some even indirectly called me a sell out all because I spoke fluent English and the white clients loved me. This found me being violated by people, I trusted to guide me, and I actually thought were like family.

There was this one time when I was waiting for my drinks order, a waiter came from behind me and pressed me against the counter; it was a busy night and it made me shrug off his actions thinking that maybe he was trying to reach for his drinks. It happened again, but the second time he whispered in my ear *why uthanda abelungu (why do you like white people?)*, I turned my head to try to look at his face and break free from his hold. He had me pinned against the wall, his manhood pressed against my backside and his breath fell disgustingly on my neck. I nudged him violently with my elbow, must have hit him in his stomach because he pulled back, groaning in pain and I walked away. His actions sent me into a wormhole that I never thought I would ever find myself in.

I trembled, I felt vulnerable and exposed as if the protective cocoon had been ripped open. I threatened to tell on him, I was ready to file a sexual assault case; first with the bosses, I did not feel safe around him and he threatened me back; promised to make my time at the restaurant hell. He would then laugh, saying that he was playing but a part of me knew that he was not lying. Something sinister was hidden in the way he laughed. One customer must have seen what he had done to me, or maybe he heard him threatening me. I remember him telling the waiter that he didn't like the way he treated me, that must have infuriated him because he started to avoid being in the same space as I was and he avoided talking to me.

My mother came to South Africa; she had to see me after the terrible migraine I had experienced. This time it was worse than most episodes, it affected my speech and my eyesight and it did not help that I was alone. This episode, did not give a warning like the other episodes I experienced, I was perfectly fine that Sunday morning. I did my shift with ease and was lucky enough to be part of the group that was chosen to knock off early. *I remember this vividly because it was one of the Sundays that the restaurant hosted buffets.* I was texting my mother on the phone as I made my way to my new place. She was still in Zimbabwe and had not planned a visit, seeing that I had just moved I had not quite settled in. I felt a terrible headache coming from the back of my neck to my forehead. The driver was playing loud music; I thought it was the reason behind my sudden head pains. I quickly asked him to stop the car, as I was a few houses away from where I stayed. I remember walking to my place with my head hanging low, it felt heavy and suddenly I could not see the pathway. My vision became blurred in one eye and I forced myself to walk fast enough so I could reach home.

When I arrived home I fumbled for my keys and opened the screen gate, by the time I was trying to open the door to my room the pain had gotten worse. I recall throwing my bag on my pump bed and I sat on the floor, it felt as though my head was expanding and I pulled out the weave I had sewn on to my head. With each pluck I felt some sort of relief, that's when I sent a voice note to my mother to tell her about the excruciating pain I was feeling, as I was talking to her on the phone all of a sudden I could not see. I became hysterical, tears flowing flooding my face. I thought I was going blind everything had gone dark. My tongue felt tied and my jaws clamped; I could not speak, I panicked, I could not send voice notes to my mother and I could not type. I remember my mother advising me to put salt under my tongue, she must have thought that I was under some spiritual attack. Black magic. Somehow, I had managed to tap the button to listen to her voice message. I fumbled for my bag; I remembered that I had a tiny packet of salt from the take-away I had ordered earlier while at work. I did as she advised and somehow my jaws loosened, but I still could not put words together to make a sentence. I was freaking out. I patted my way into the bathroom and turned on the faucet to splash some cold water onto my face, at this point I had forgotten there was a sink that had a tap right outside my door. After a few splashes of water on my face I gained vision in my right eye, the dark cloud was thinning away; with my one good eye I texted my mother, since I still could not speak properly. She told me to pray, and I did. The more I prayed the more the pain in my head fought back, I wanted to scream but I knew that no one was going to come to my rescue. After what seemed to be an hour or so, the headache cleared and slowly my vision returned together with my speech but I was weak. I fell asleep instantly forgetting to lock the door, it was as if I had passed out. I remember gaining consciousness and everything was dark, I had woken up from a dream where my father came to me with some bananas, I ate a few and was jolted up from the dream. When I was up, I felt hungry and remembered that my landlord had a tuck-shop. I dashed out, with a wobble in my knees and saw her coming out of the bath and the first thing I asked her was if she had any bananas. Her Spaza shop only sold packed goods like chips, biscuits, sugar, rice, and juice among other things; I stumbled back into my room, threw myself on to the bed, and slept. When I woke up in the morning, my head was numb; it felt as though it had suddenly deflated. I texted my mother and she were relieved to hear from me.

Thus, a month later my mother came to my place. Seemed so much easier; talking to her, saving up for rent and finally I could eat properly. When she came she found me with a sandwich maker that I had begged my uncle, (*My father's youngest uncle, he too stayed in Cosmo city)* to give me. I was planning on using it to cook eggs and making sandwiches until I eventually save enough for a stove after I had paid rent. This seemed impossible before my mother came, as I had to save R1500 for rent and another thousand for transport and the remainder for food. I had managed to buy an electric kettle, which meant I could have a proper hot bowl of porridge and a cup of tea and a sandwich. But when mom came, she changed all that. After getting a job, she got us a two-plate stove on her first paycheck and my uncle (my father's youngest brother) bought me a set of pots; *a kind of housewarming gift.* It all began to fall in place.

Chapter 26

The woman who sat on table eight some months ago came back, and coincidentally she was my customer and sat on the same table as the last time. She was different, a lot different from the last time she was at the restaurant. She had a clean-shaven head and her make-up was not as messy as the last time. She looked happier, and smiled a lot. She came with a male companion, he also looked friendly; I wondered if it was her husband or boyfriend considering the fact that she had nothing good to say about her husband.
"*Hello dear, can you get me juice? What brand juices do you have?*" She did not give me time to greet them and introduce myself. We all seemed like we were programmed to do that, surely it was part of our training, to smile, greet, and introduce ourselves. It was beginning to become a bit inhumane. The male companion noticed how she had cut me off,
"*Thembi, she hasn't done her robotic greeting; you know they have to do that or else they won't get paid.*" He chuckled as he placed his phone on the table after switching it off. I learnt what the woman's name was, I could not continue with my 'robotic' introduction I just smiled and waited for the man to place his order. The woman, whom I now knew her name was Thembi, looked at me, scanning as if she were looking for something.
"*Oh my God, dear!*" she screamed. "*This is the girl I told you about, the one who looked after me some months back.*" I questioned whether this man was her husband or not. She possibly could not have told her husband about her drinking spree as well as her counselling session with me; *I thought.*
"*Wow! You have changed, you look a lot healthier.*" I felt a little offended, but she was not lying, I had changed from the last time she saw me. I had stopped wearing three pairs of pants under my jeans to hold them up, the protruding cheekbones that made me look like Emily from the corpse bride had disappeared, and so did the boney neckline. I finally had a little flesh on my bones, most importantly, my smile was not forced, and it came naturally on its own.

"*Honey, you can't say that about other people.*" The man looked at his switched off phone. I smiled and placed the menus on the table, "*it is okay, after that night she can get away with anything. Besides she is not lying.*" I gave a tiny giggle, I did not want them to feel like they had offended me even though I was terrible embarrassed about her remark. I was glad that no one else apart from the three of us heard the comment. Thembi laughed with me as well, "*THIS is the husband I told you about, and thanks to you we sorted our issues.*" She gave me a wink. I wondered what the wink meant, was it to stop me from continuing the story or it was meant for me to smile and congratulate them, I chose the latter. The man looked at both of us in awe, he seemed not to know the whole story, and I thought it was best to keep it that way. They seemed happy and that was good.
"*We have Mr Juice brand, Orange, Mango, and Tropical flavors,*" I went back to her first question avoiding what could have become an awkward moment. She winked again as

she sat back in her chair, *"Ummmm, get me a mango juice first and will see if I can keep it down."* She said and she placed her hand on her tummy, I noticed but chose to ignore her gesture. *"I will have a Hunter's dry,"* the man placed his order while staring at the menu. Moments later I returned with their drinks order, they gave me their food orders, and quickly I went to place their order. While I was busy giving the kitchen explanation of the instructions I had written, Thembi came looking for me. I went to her smiling, hoping that she did not want to change her order.

"I really meant what I said a while back, you really do look happy now." She placed her hand on my shoulders.

"I can say I'm less stressed, I am staying on my own, and my mother is this side now." I told her. She now felt like a close friend, as if I could tell her anything.

"That day you didn't tell me anything but in my drunken state I could tell that you had a lot troubling you." She paused and looked in the direction of her table as if she was worried that her husband was going to see us talking.

"Prayers are answered dear, they seem to take long, but they come at the right time. We, humans we are just quick to quit." She said. I started to think of the time I almost quit life and joined the dead. I was down and out and ready to tap out without waiting for the answers I was praying for.

"My prayers were finally answered; after that night I quit drinking and had a frank chat with HIM, he listened. I'm going to be a mother in a few months." She placed her hand on her small baby bump that was barely visible unless you squinted and zoomed in for a closer look.

"Some things are good to quit, but do not quit on life." She smiled. I congratulated her on her baby news and she left for her table. She seemed to be pleased with herself and she deserved to be, she had triumphed in what seemed to be the greatest battle of her life and she was soon to be bringing one more person into the world. I felt good about myself that day; I do not know why because all I did was to give her alcohol and listen to her complain about something that I had no experience in helping. Sometimes listening is all that is needed, and I wanted that too; someone who would listen without judging or telling me what to do. It felt like I expected too much, I had succumbed to my thoughts and had a spiritual gift to deal with and did not know how to do so.

Chapter 27

With my mother with me in South Africa, everything seemed easy in a way. The one person I could talk to was closer to me and I did not feel quite alone as before. My uncle (my father's youngest brother) found her work at his old friend's place, basic housework that required her to stay over at her boss's place, she seemed thrilled to have something to do, and it gave me solace, anything that made her happy gave me happiness. She would get off days during the weekends and sometimes I took off days on Sundays and would spend the day window shopping and just having a fun time.
Now that there was a little more happiness in my life than before, I stressed less. I became more open and it is funny how good old things, or should I say people from the past pop up when you think positively and do things with a positive mind.
My first crush had reached out to me on Facebook. I was on my way to work, and his message rekindled a fire that had long been extinguished. We spoke, and each time I was reminded of how I used to feel about him, when he was still in Varsity and I was still a high school baby. I knew that he would never give me a second look, there were much prettier girls at Varsity than I was so I never told him; I never told anyone. His text brought back the old vulnerable Liz, one who had turned sixteen and started to discover new things about herself. I fell in love with him all over again, but I was not sure if he felt the same way about me; of course, I had bloomed into a young woman, curves and all but was I finally in his 'league of women'?

We started talking on the phone, became acquainted, and grew closer. My work friend, Lihle was the first one to see this change in me, as I would sneak into the bathroom every time he called just to avoid being caught by my bosses talking on the phone. I would come out of the bathroom with a smile plastered on my face; I liked this new feeling I had finally found. I forgot that I was different, that I heard voices speaking to me. The singer, who said *who do you tell when you love someone,* must have had me in mind when they wrote the song. I wanted to tell my mother, my one true confidante but could not. I was terrified, this was the one thing I couldn't tell her, the one time I found a different kind of happy I couldn't share it with her. I would look at her and create the conversation in my head, surely, I was childish to think that I would be reprimanded for dating at my age; most girls even started dating younger. I kept This love I felt to myself, for as long as I could, until one day he asked me out for a date. He was going to be in South Africa; I recall being excited to be near him, and I was excited to see if what I felt for him was real.

I remember sitting with my mother in our room while a movie was playing on my laptop. I peeked over her, stealing glances and trying gauge how her mood was. The last thing I wanted was to make her angry. When my mother caught me staring at her, the question I dreaded followed,
"what is wrong, Lizzy?" my heart started beating fast as I thought of ways to perfectly

phrase my answer. I started wondering about her response, a part of me thought she was going to scold me_ but for what reason, I had no answer to.
I recall putting my phone on silent, to avoid any calls that could come through and disturb 'the talk'. I looked at her intently, still thinking of a way to start my story.
"*Do you remember that boy we met in Harare*?" I have no idea what I was thinking starting my story like that, but it was the only way I could start the story. I figured that if I began it like that and gradually come to the main point she would have cooled down by the time I was finished talking.
"*What boy in Harare*?" She frowned and wrinkles formed on her forehead. Something she always does when she is paying attention.
"*You know, when we went to dad's friend a year after the funeral*." I paused waiting for her reaction.
"*The one who was sitting in the car when we arrived?*" she inquired. I was stunned that she remembered something from seven years.
"*No, I mean the elder brother, the one who was in varsity, the taller one*." I gave a vague description. I did not want her to know quickly how smitten I was; that he was not just tall, he was dark, and now had a buff body, quite developed from the last time I saw him when I was still invisible to him. He had a dimple that graced his face whenever he smiled; I noticed it then and had noticed now when we had a video chat. He had a baritone voice that gave off a manly aura I was definitely not immune to. I didn't want her know, how I got butterflies every time he sent me a message and how I smiled every time he came to my thoughts.
"*Oh! That one, what about him?*" she questioned. Now the time had come for me to tell her. "*Well we have been talking on the phone for a while now and he says he works for a company that is based here in S.A*." I know I should have told her the main reason why I had reminded her about him, but I still had not found the right words. I gathered my courage as I took a deep breath, I saw her getting impatient, and probably she wanted to get back to her movie. As I exhaled, I blurted out everything I wanted her to know at one go.

"*We had been talking and he said he liked me and I think I like him too*." I stopped, I know I should not have said 'I think', but was the only way I could avoid any other awkward questions. I knew that I more than liked him.
"*Oh? How long have you two been talking?*" she asked, this time looking at me.
"*It's been a while, some months*." I said,
"*How old is he by the way*?" I felt relief slowly creeping in as I told her that he was four years older than I was. I remember my mother being super chilled about the whole idea of me having a boyfriend; it became easier for me when I told her about the date that I had to go on. The conversation I had with my mother, even though it was awkward gave me a settling feeling; I felt unjudged and loved. Something I had been yearning since I came to South Africa. The feeling that rose within me was might have been caused by her knowing about my newfound love, but was something that had been waiting to come out for a long time.
I remember feeling nervous on the first date. I was finally going to spend time with a

person that I had been in love with for a long time. I tried to keep myself calm and collected; I needed him not to see how nervous he made me feel. We met at a Mall in Randburg, and my nerves took the better of me; my knees were like jelly and I had to take in deep breaths secretly just so I would not pass out. We went inside a pizza place; I remember not eating, I could not. My tummy must have been full with all the butterflies I had harbored. The day was perfect, except for the awkward pizza moment. He walked me to the taxi rank as I was going to an opposite direction from his, he gave me a hug as we parted and kissed me on the forehead. As I watched him walking away, I let out an almost loud exhale and felt the nerves escape, and I was my normal self again.

After the date, we maintained contact for months and he kept a smile on my face during that time. I finally felt like my peers, I finally proved that I was not as weird as I thought I was. Then it began, the time for my happiness to be shattered, I was at work when suddenly break up songs started playing on the radio and a feeling that something bad was going to happen sneaked up on me. I took my earphones and plugged them into my ears, and continued to clean. As I listened to the songs on my phone, I kept getting the feeling that I was going to get bad news; I started feeling emotional to the point that I took my earphones and ripped them up into pieces. The next day I was not working, had a perfectly planned day but my communication with 'my boyfriend' was rather cold, but I assumed that it could have been because we were both busy. The next day I was off, it was during the week and my mother was at work. I remember being busy cleaning and tidying up my room, as I did my chores I was talking to him and everything seemed fine until he sent me the text that broke me.

He sent me a long text message telling me how he had to deal with himself and could not continue to date me. I remember my heart stopping and tears gushing down my face. The more I wiped them off the more they came flooding my face. When I finally could feel my heart beating, it had a sharp pain piercing through it. I did not want anything to do with him; he had broken my heart and once again made me feel worthless. I recall crying, blaming the gift that I had; a part of me felt as if it was the reason behind the break-up. That is when I started feeling as if no one could ever love a weird girl who heard voices speaking to her and saw visions of weird things. When my mother finally got wind of the break up three days later, she was the pillow I needed that gave me some sort of comfort. I was certain that I was never going to let anyone hurt me the way he did. I hated the gift; it felt as though it was out to destroy my life and had me wondering if ever I would find anyone that would not be scared of what I had.

It felt as though I hallucinated every feeling that I had for him. I thought that it was the 'gift's fault, a curse it would seem; taking everything that I cared for and hindering happiness from finding me.

Chapter 28

I think you look pretty.
The words from the first ever note I got from a white man, crumbled inside the bill folder. The letters were crooked as though he was running while he was writing it, but it was cute in way and it brought a smile to my face. He had asked for a piece of paper, I should have known that was his mission. It had been months since I had gotten my heart broken and never thought that I would ever feel it beat in this manner again. I was your plain Jane; never spiced up my uniform like the other female waiters, I tucked my green golf shirt in my work jeans and wore the assigned 'All Star' black tennis shoes. I was invisible until he came to my section and gave me that note. I remember trying to shrug off the excitement that came with a white man complimenting me; not that other clients didn't call me beautiful or good looking which I always questioned since I did not look like Carol or the other prettier waitress who wore make up. I always thought I was invisible.

He would stare at me, not creepily, but in a more lustful and seductive way. My naïve eyes would connect with his, a shade of green with a tinge of blue, like an ocean during a rainy summer afternoon as I stole glances at him and immediately shy away. His blonde hair was perfectly cut with just a few strands caressing his forehead; he would reveal his manly smile as he flicked the stubborn hairs from his face. He would do it playfully as if he knew that I was peeking over him. I am sure he knew that I had seen the note; it was in the way he smiled each time he looked my way. I went back to his table, wearing a smile on my face and pretended as if I had not seen the note, he would smile back; he did not come off as one of the perverts that I had to fight off on most busy nights. He apologized for writing the note *if it had offended me in any way*. How could such a note offend me? I thought it was cute; *the way the paper was crumbled and his crooked handwriting.* It was definitely not offensive in any way, unlike the others who used to hound me. He asked to know more about myself, there was something about the way he was interested in knowing me. He took small sips and had his full attention to me, as if he was listening to the sounds that came out as I spoke and all the while he smiling with his chin resting on his right palm. He asked if I could write my number on the back of the bill; I stood by the machine, contemplating on whether I should go ahead with it. He seemed harmless and I did not want to seem rude, I also did not want any of my work colleagues finding out about what I was debating on doing. I took a paper from my waiter's notebook, jotted down my number and my name without any of my colleagues noticing, and slid it in the bill folder together with the bill. I remember him placing his hand on mine as I placed the folder on his table; I remember his hand feeling warm on top of mine and he asked me, *did you?* I pulled back my hand, smiled and walked away. I stood by the bar, hidden and looked at him. He did not open the folder in a hurry; instead, he took a sip of the last drop of beer left in his glass and stared at the TV that was mounted just above the bar. He looked sad, almost disappointed, I wondered if the piece of paper with my number had somehow been lost in transit. I went back to the table with the swipe machine; I kept my smile plastered on my face. I realized that he had not opened the folder, *he must have been nervous* I thought. He smiled and opened the folder and took out his wallet, he lifted the bill and saw the paper with my number. His face lit up, like a kid in a candy store; he paid up his bill and left. He texted me the moment he disappeared in his red Volvo.

Jason was an insurance broker at least that is what he told me and the other customers he met when he came to the restaurant. He always made sure that he gave anyone he met his business card, though a part of me was bothered by the fact that he spent almost half his time at the restaurant. He would bring his paperwork sometimes in the mornings and make calls here and there; I shrugged off the idea of him lying about his work. He was Afrikaans, but different from the other Afrikaans nationals I had met; he was much friendlier and more humane. I liked the attention I got from him, made me forget the 'curse' and being around him often I grew to like him. He would check on me after I knock off and sometimes show up early at the restaurant just to see me before work. We became close, I fell in love and he must have too; even though I remember second guessing myself every time he gave me a kiss, of course we had to hide our relationship because he did not want me to lose my job and I could not bear the embarrassment of being fired for fraternizing with clients. I especially did not want my uncles finding out, it would have been worse if I had gotten myself fired because of Jason.

Being with Jason was not because of the money, or because he was white, though I had already seen my escape from a life that was suffocating. I liked the attention he gave me. Sure, he was older, I was twenty-two, and he was thirty-three I did not see anything wrong with it, I had already had my heart broken by a younger man I thought I had saved myself the heartache. Whenever he came to my workplace and we would steal some minutes, and chat away either by his table or by his car. I had not told him about the gift that was haunting me; I was terrified that it would scare him off.
He seemed perfect until one day he hit me with a surprise that raised a huge red flag that I chose to ignore, the first of many. He introduced me to his sons; *not one but* two adorable little boys that came with their father half-asleep. I did not know how to react this was the second time I had dated anyone and the first time I ever experienced this. He sat in the booth that was used as the waiter's station and woke the boys up, one was about four and the other was two; immediately I wondered about their mother, my heart started to pound all of a sudden I grew scared. He had never told me about the boys, even when I had asked about him being married he had said that he was not. I was smitten and that put me in a trap, I wondered if I was able to be a stepmother at twenty-two that too to two boys overnight. A part of me thought that he was serious about me, hence he introduced me to his children, but the spiritual side of me screamed and waived many red flags that I certainly would not miss.

I meditated on the issue, something that I had learnt to do if I wanted to connect with my higher self and find answers. This was something I should have done the moment I started to become close to him. I found none; except for more red flags and doubt, it must have been because I wanted to manipulate the situation to suit what I wanted. I thought I could ignore the warnings I was getting, I hated my job, and it felt like I was robbed off my childhood. I had to bear the embarrassment of being called 'Aunty' which was term used by spoiled white kids to call their maids, I had to go through being summoned by children half my age and pretend to be happy to serve them just for them to tip me five rand if I'm lucky ten. I had dreams to further my education, become a lawyer or a psychiatrist or something that was respectable, but I was stuck in a job that exposed me to drunks, drug addicts, and prostitutes. Jason seemed like the answer that I needed even though I was steps away to being a stepmother at twenty-two, it did not seem as bad as it sounded did; considering the worst, I was already facing.

Feeling that my 'gift' had dumped me to deal with the Jason issue, it was not clear enough for me and so I sought other options. I interrogated him further and he said with ease that he had divorced the mother of his kids. My instincts questioned his answer, his children were small it would have been impossible for them to divorce; but then again divorce was a popular thing in South Africa. He started acting weird, ghosting me and chatting less on the phone. My instincts went with the fact that he might have gotten back together with the mother of his children. I had not told my mother about the children, I knew she would have discouraged me against dating him, which I was not sure of anymore. Jason came to the restaurant one night and told me about his house he had just bought and wanted to show me on an estate. I told my mother of the 'date', I already had an off day from work; this was going to be the first time I was going to see Jason outside of the restaurant, and I was scared. I had started not trust him well enough to be with him alone, heck he sprung the kids on me. I meditated on the 'date', googled the place I was going to be and save his number on my mother's phone just in case anything happened to me. I remember pacing up and down my tiny room waiting for his call, and surely, his call came through. He was cancelling the date; his youngest son had fallen off a tree and wounded his chin, relief coursed through me. My spirit guide had come through for me, I asked for a way out and it happened; at the expense of a child but it happened. Though a part of me was disappointed of the fact that he had cancelled a date I had dressed up for, I had found the answers I wanted.

Then he ghosted me some more, he stopped texting and coming to the restaurant. One cold Tuesday, the restaurant was dead quiet; only a few people came through for tea and coffee, which were not tippers. I went upstairs and sat in one of the dusty booths we had forgotten to clean that day. I connected my phone to the WIFI and started to browse my Facebook feed. Something suddenly came over me and felt the urge to search for Jacob on Facebook; I fumbled for his business card that I had tucked away in my pink billabong purse. I typed up his surname in the search box looking at each letter carefully on the card as I typed; his Afrikaans surname was difficult for me to memorize. While I waited for the loading circle to stop turning and show me the results, I questioned my actions; was I going to be able to handle whatever I was going to see on his page? When I was about to answer myself, his name popped up first on the list I clicked on the profile picture, and it led me to his Facebook feed. I started to scroll down, I do not know what I was looking for, but I needed answers to his sudden Houdini act. Then I saw it; the post that shattered me into pieces, he was celebrating his anniversary with the mother of his children; he even wrote a message for her. I quickly logged out and went straight down stairs. I could not control my tears; I had been duped.

Days after I had finally gathered myself, working through the tears and forcing smiles, which I was now an expert at doing. He walked in, and I saw him chatting with the waiters that were standing by the entrance. I heard one of the waiters confirm that I was available, I was not happy about that but it was not his fault, no one at the restaurant knew about my fling or should I call it an affair considering what I had found out. He walked through to the bar area and sat by a barrel that was next to the miniature fountain. I tried to avoid him as much as I could, he got his usual drink from the bartender, and I could not care less. I felt a volcano about to erupt within me; I could not find the right words to say to him, I was just too hurt.
"Lizzy I gave your customer his castle lite but did not ring it up, please do that on your tab." The bartender called out to me as I checked the order on my new table. I was not fond of early customers as they made it hard for me to finish my cleaning duty and they rarely tipped. Most importantly, I was not happy with Jason being the first customer I served. Jason was sitting at the spot where I was supposed to clean, most of my cleaning stuff was still there, and had to remove it before Marcus came through, and I tried to get some of my colleagues to remove them for me with much failure. Reluctantly I went to the table, to get my stuff obviously. I knew he was going to try to speak to me, he did not know that I had found out about the part of his life that was a secret to me.
"*Hie Liz, you look beautiful today*." He smiled looking at me affectionately.
"*Hie, Thanks. Do you want another beer?*" I asked, picking up the gloves and brush I was going to use to clean the fountain.
"*Yes please.*" Before he could say anything more, I walked away and rung up the order including the first one that the bartender had given him.
"*Malume, don't give me two, the other one is the beer you gave him*." I told the bartender as he was about to pour a second glass of the draught beer.
"*Okay Mshana.*" I called him uncle as a sign of respect and he reciprocated that by addressing me as his niece. I felt my smile fade away as I approached Jason's table, he had already gone through his first beer.
"*You don't look okay, are you not feeling well?*" I could sense concern in his voice, but I could not shrug of the fact that he was lying to me and hiding things from me.
"*I'm okay*." I grabbed the glass with my right hand with my tray under my left armpit. He grabbed the hand that had the glass.
"*Babe, I can tell that you are not okay*." He brushed my arm with his other hand. I felt a cold shiver go up my spine and hives covered the hand that he was caressing. I freed my hand from his grip and looked into his eyes and the green in his eyes glimmered. He looked as someone who was not hiding anything.
"*I'm okay*." I frowned as I rubbed down the hives. "*Is it because I wasn't here for New Year's?*" I could not believe that he thought that I was angry with him not being around on New Year's amongst all the things.
"*I don't want to talk about that, besides I'm busy.*" He grabbed my hand again and begged

me to talk to him. After he noticed that I was not budging he paid for his drinks and left. He sent me a text, asking me if I was okay and if he could see me again.

I agreed only because I wanted to see his face when I asked him about what I saw on his Facebook account. He came, full with confidence smiling as he always did. It was noon, and freezing cold, I was with chatting with the kitchen staff while my friend made tea for herself. A text came through my phone and I went to the toilet to answer it. It was him, telling me that he had been sitting in the smoking section for a while. I went up to him and he asked how I feeling.

"*Why did you lie to me?*" the question came out unexpectedly.

"*Lie?*" He sunk into his chair and placed his phone on the table. "*What did I lie about?*" my heart started to pound, and I felt my eyes well up. I pulled myself together and gathered all that I could so that I could find out what I already knew.

"*I saw that you were celebrating your anniversary, congratulations*." I took a deep inhale and silently exhaled the air I had taken in.

"*Oh that is what you were mad about in the morning, Hun that is just for the kids. To give them some sort of normalcy.*" As he tried to explain himself, I could tell that he was lying.

"*Jase, they are too young to know about all that stuff, well done you fooled me. I cannot do this anymore.*" I folded my hands across my chest.

I was done with whatever fling we had, I could not afford the embarrassment. He tried to beg me to understand, hoping that maybe I would ignore everything and pretend as if I had seen nothing. It was difficult for me to do so. He said goodbye and it was the last I saw of him.

Chapter 29

"Hello there may I have somewhere quiet I can work?"
His blue-grey eyes shone through the restaurant lights. *"We have an upstairs, no one is sitting there tonight, or you can have one of the booths in the non-smoking section. It is a bit quiet there."* I responded to his request to which he took the second option and I helped him to his table. He sat in the corner booth, pounding away on the keyboard with the backlight in his eyes and he stared passionately on the computer screen. I knew he was making headway with whatever he was, typing as his face gave off a satisfied look. He never once looked at me as I gave him his Amstel Beer. I remember walking up to him and peeking over to look at what he was busy with, I saw words, thousands of them, and I glanced at him as he smiled, pleased with himself for what he had produced. I had a sudden I crave for the feelings that he was exuding, I wanted to feel the same passion he felt at that moment. The pixelated words on his blue screen spoke to me, even though I could not tell what was written but I wanted more of the bug that had bitten me.

"Looks like you are enjoying your work, can I get you another drink?" I initiated small talk as I found out if he wanted another drink. I asked him about his writing, his voice spewed excitement like an active volcano. We spoke about writing and books; it was heartwarming talking to someone about something different. I found it strange that he was the second person to encourage me to write as a form of therapy, though he did not say it in that much words. I was slowly being beckoned to a world that I certainly had no interest in but the call was loud and it was only a matter time until I accepted the call. Just like the gift.
"Here, take my business card." He handed me a small rectangular card with his surname on it with the word attorneys at the end. Craig was a lawyer, a passionate painter, and a writer. He came to the restaurant almost every night before this, with his laptop and tap away for hours on end; this was the first time I spoke to him. He was tall; his height was visible even while he was lounged in the booths. Strands of his blonde hair would fall on his forehead and his eyes lit up every time he wrote.
I remember having a lengthy conversation with him, stealing moments in-between my other tables. He was much more interesting than the other three tables I had, and he too seemed keen to converse with me.

Even if I wanted to write or to be a writer like him, I did not have it in me. I barely had the time to write, working almost sixteen hours every day need I mention the time to socialize outside of work. It became a dream, stashed away in another pile of things I wished to do and I envied that he was living this dream. I would drift away as I watched him tap on the keys from a distance; it looked like he was in a different world from the one we were in and wondered how it felt like to escape. It was all I wanted, to find an escape and be free of all things that were burdening me. *Was that too much to ask?*

Chapter 30

I saw a bulldozer knocking down one side of the restaurant, and dust choked the air. I walked down to the kiddies section and I saw the slide being pulled out and the floors being drilled up. The noise of construction filled my ears and the dust stuffed my nose, then suddenly a familiar voice called out to me, forcing its way into the ruckus. Another boring Tuesday saw me phasing out into what had become my comfort zone. *"Lizzy, your table needs you!"* amid the noise, I heard a familiar voice. I stared into the direction where it came from and saw a fellow waiter standing by the entrance stairs. I slowly zoned in, there was no construction, the walls and the floors were all still intact so were the slides. Right there and then I realized that I had experienced another vision. I walked to my table, confused about what I had just seen. As I walked away from my table, a voice spoke to me, *"did you see what is coming?"* I looked around to see if there was anyone near me. It spoke again, *"you will have to leave Dros, it will be close down soon."* At this stage, I had mastered communicating with the voice telepathically, the only way that avoided awkwardness with people. I asked the voice where I would go and tried to negotiate that I needed the job and the voice responded, *"You will be told in due course, what you just saw will start in a few weeks' time."* I felt depressed, sitting by the stairs; I was warming up to the job and now I was I being told to move. I thought to share the news with my friends, hoping to hear what good ideas they might have. *"Guys, do you know that Marcus is planning to knock this place down?"* I did not calculate their possible reaction to my absurd news. I looked at their faces and they responded with laughter. As they were laughing Marcus came in and dragged Charlie to the side and they spoke for a long while as we kept ourselves busy to avoid being in trouble with the boss. There was an eerie silence between them, and then almost immediately we were called in to an emergency meeting upstairs. We settled in the chairs and stared blankly at Marcus, I already knew what was coming, *"I'm going to be closing shop for a while, for renovations and when it opens it might not be Dros."* There were gasps filling the air, he continued, *"we will contact you guys on what you will do next, we will close in a few weeks."* With those words, he left the building. My friends looked at me in awe; I had told them something that actually came true. They tried questioning me, trying to find out how I knew about what Marcus had said and I did not know how to explain to them. I was scared they would call me crazy if not a witch.

Later that night I sat in our taxi as we waited for other waiters who had not quite finished cashing up. Thoughts about where I was going to be next flooded my mind, I tried to negotiate with my thoughts; surely, I did not have to leave, the restaurant was surely going to open again. The voice fought with my thoughts, I was supposed to leave. *"save the money you have and return to Zimbabwe."* the voice said and I felt like I was at cross roads, I didn't want to fight with my spirit guide it helped me with everything I faced but now it was telling me to quit, the one thing I never wanted to do. Quitting South Africa would mean that I would have failed, I would not get that 'proud of you' smile from my uncle, and he would only see me as a quitter and failure. I was told to stop going to the restaurant, whenever I tried to disobey, I would have trouble getting a taxi until it was too late. They had already closed the place anyways, all they wanted was the waiters to clean the place up and pack up the equipment. The days grew closer and my stay in South Africa was numbered, I had saved up enough money, together with mom but we had bought a whole lot of stuff while we were there I was worried we wouldn't be able to get them through the boarder. When Craig heard about my sudden trip back home, he helped me with money to add to our transport fare. Even though this was fool proof, I questioned everything I was doing; I questioned my stay in Zimbabwe, and what was I going to do there? I had been staying in South Africa for three years and I had lost all contacts of my father's friends. If I never left, I would have had a job easy straight after school.

It felt defeated, and betrayed. It felt as though my gift was turning into a curse and ruining my life; here I was scared to argue with the spirits. When my uncle came to our place, and showed his disapproval on us leaving South Africa I felt scared. This was the second biggest leap I was taking into the unknown; I know it might sound like Zimbabwe was now a stranger to me, it was more than that, I had run away from everything there and it felt like everything was waiting for me at my doorstep.
There I was sitting in a rumbling bus, heart throbbing; was I taking the right decision?
"Mom, are you sure you want us to do this?" I asked my mother as the bus growled with smoke covering the air.
"Lizzy, Angel has never strayed you. There must be a reason why we have to go to Zimbabwe; I would listen to her if I were you." She looked at me just as a lioness would look at her cubs. *"But what about uncle..."* I tried to find a reason that could come as an excuse but she interjected before I could finish. *"You should start trusting your instincts and your spirit guide."* She was right; I needed to start living my life, at least what I had. I needed to stop trying to please people, but it was easier said than done. The last passenger climbed onto the bus and the driver followed, as the bus made its way out of Power house_ a somewhat make shift station where buses to Zimbabwe parked. Loud conversations in Shona muffled my thinking voice, the more I head the other passengers speak the more I wanted to be in Zimbabwe. The rumbling bus said otherwise, it became a battle between my heart and my head, one that never ends. I closed my eyes and said a prayer, I felt like I was defying my uncle and doing what I dreaded the most_ disappointing him.
"*Is it your instruction that we leave South Africa for Zimbabwe?"* I asked my spirit guide one more time. At this moment, I could clearly hear her and dreams were much clearer as well. I had mastered the art of meditation, channeling, and telepathy.
"*Yes, as instructed by God."* She responded.
"*What do you feel?"* she asked. I kept my eyes closed, listened to the humming of the engine and the rustle of the items in the bus as the conductors packed them in the boot.
"I feel terrified." I answered.
"*That's good; know that feeling, remember it, it will always guide you when you are stuck in making decisions."* She spoke, and I opened my eyes, my brow furrowed I was in utter confusion. *"Every time you get a scared feeling, know that it's the right thing to do."* I

questioned this, how could something scary be a good decision?
That was when I realized that the fear was different; that of bad news caused my heart to throb, and the fear that my spirit guide spoke about made my tummy turn. As confusing as it was, this was first time I understood how the whole gift thing worked. This fear that I felt in my tummy pushed me towards something I was supposed to do and most times that thing would be good for me. The other fear pushed me away from danger.

The bus coughed its way out of Johannesburg, and my mother could not stop worrying about her microwave that was placed at the backseat of the bus with other people's goods. She made sure that the conductor placed her property safely and she would take glances at the stuff making sure nothing had fallen out of place. If she had her way, she would have traveled the whole trip with her microwave on her lap and the T.V stand under her seat. The conductor had convinced her countless times that her stuff was safe, only for him to give up and allow her to do periodic inspections. I on the other hand switched off my phone, I had not told my work mates about my impromptu travel plans; I don't know why, I guess I didn't want them judging me. They too would have disapproved of my choice, they did not understand me, and they would have never understood that a spirit guide told me to up and leave, heck I did not understand it but I trusted her.

Chapter 31

I was finally leaving South Africa, a place where I felt trapped, even though I could have left at any given time. I was in a dungeon with fire breathing dragons, burning me at every given second. Silently I took the hits and silently they broke me, but now I was finally going to be free and it was as scary as hell. Who knew freedom could be this scary? I guess it is how prisoners feel when they finally get out.
The yellow bus raced against the setting sun, I thought the bus driver was working with my spirit guide to get me out of South Africa as soon as possible, but he just wanted to arrive at the border before it was pitch dark. The border was a stressful place for everyone involved, the paper work that had to be done took up most of the time, especially if one's passport had issues, like overstayed, or expired. Just like my mothers', she had overstayed due to the job and mine_ well it had that fake permit and it claimed that I had returned to Zimbabwe long back. We had our luggage to worry about; we needed to declare it and we were not sure if we had enough money to declare them. My mother was hopeful that we were going cross the border smoothly. We arrived at the border some hours later, it was dark; some said it was the best time to cross the border, to me it was few metres away from my escape from South Africa. We were instructed to disembark from the bus with our entire luggage that we were meant to declare.
"*Each person should stand by their items and fill in this form.*" The conductor said as he handed us tiny declaration forms. I did the paper work while my mother checked if we still had all our stuff. The immigration officer, for border control came to a woman who was next to me and checked the stuff she had. After the thorough check he went to a man who was on the other side of the bus, ignoring me. I was stunned by his actions and annoyed, the man had not declared everything he had, and they made him leave a car engine that was part of the undeclared items. He maintained the skipping routine and I was feeling irritated, he then checked the stuff that was with my mother on the other side of the bus and she told him that the other half was with me when he came to me he instructed me to close my bags and ticked the checked box. Startled by his actions I looked at him, he had barely looked at the items I had.
"*Put everything back on the bus*." He instructed as he walked away, my mother came to me and called out to him thinking that I had not declared any of the stuff.
"It's all good ma'am" he walked away to the next bus. We put the bags back on the bus and took our seats, when everyone was settled the driver cranked the engine and we were on our way. As for our passports, no one asked for it, everything went smoothly and just like that, we were back home. I had to deal with all of my fears, my nightmares, and my pain. I had run away only to go back and face it all.
There was a different feeling that came with this return, far different from my other visits.

Some nights after our arrival, I had a dream; drums beckoned me to a rural setting. It was though they were celebratory drums. I walked towards a round hut; it seemed familiar, as

I entered the room, I saw old people sitting in a circle with their backs against the call of the mud hut. I looked around the room as I entered and one of the old people guided me to the centre of the room, I could not see a familiar face at first but I felt as though I knew all of them. The drums grew louder, I tried to look for the person banging it, but I could not see anything. There was a strong odour of snuff and traditional beer, and almost instantly, they were in front of me. One of the people in the room with me took the clay pot, passed it around, and did the same with the snuff. I started sneezing without passing it under my nose. They ululated and clapped their hands. When I looked up, scanning the room; then I saw him, my grandfather. He was sitting amongst them, suddenly I felt happier and safer. We were sitting outside all of a sudden and my grandfather was sitting with the other elders, as if they were talking and I was with the women. Like a huge wave taking over me, I knew who I was; finally, I had found my identity…

The question that remained was how was I going to show this being to people and were they going to accept me?

Chapter 32

Mornings in Zimbabwe were peaceful. Of course, a ruckus of people banging doors heading to God knows where, neighbors sharing pleasantries and dishing out the gossip bowl complimented the morning air. Ahh! Home it was everything I had missed. My spirit guide had told me to come here and here I was. *Spirit guide do not disappoint me.*

We started a clothing business, ordered a bale of clothes from Mozambique; neither of us went, my aunty *(mum's sister in-law)* did us the favor and got us the order. Selling was easy, I had my experience selling at the restaurant and mum was great with people. Quite a tag team, it got us through the day, month, and year. I was worried though, I still had not made a name for myself, and I still had not proved to my uncles that I could be someone in this said life.
I started sending out CVs; the first place I mailed my CV was the hospital. General Hospital the last place I saw my father alive. I never planned to step my foot there let alone work there, but I had no choice, I needed my uncles to be proud of me. Already we were under fire due to our abrupt departure from S.A. I avoided chatting to my uncles on Whatsapp, dreaded their phone calls, and felt like running away each time they visited. I was feeling worse than the time I was in South Africa; do not get me wrong I fit perfectly back home in Zimbabwe, despite the constant questions *why did you leave S.A? You guys should not have come back.* I could easily handle strangers asking me that question, but not my uncles. They always dropped a bomb like question on me, *what is your plan?* In turn, I would cry, secretly of course; I would never let them see my tears; if they did see them, they might have forced themselves out of my eye sockets, maybe trying to rescue me. I did not want to get married, at least not yet, not until I had proved my worth. *What was my plan?* I had one, and No it did not involve marriage. My plan was simple, create a name for myself, and prove my worth. How was I going to do that? Now that question needed answering. I was trying my best, selling clothes, sending out CVs and being a good girl. They could not see that, how could they? I hid all that seemed like I was failing.

The hospital never called, maybe they never got my application; *lost in the mail I guess.* I started going to workshops, the first one I was invited by someone close to the family, my aunt *im certain of that.* Held at Gweru's very own Regency Hotel once known as Fairmile Motel, *they pay good money* he said and *there is lunch.* This was a workshop on health, hosted by the city council and health practitioners. I sat in the hotel's dining area with thirty to fifty strangers, the hosts gave their presentations; I was bored. Kept looking at the agenda wondering when we were going to get to the payment. I had shown up and listened, they had me taking notes about something I did not care about. Grub time, we gobbled down the tasty hotel treats; I was hungry but my hunger could not be satiated by a plate of rice, chicken and coleslaw with apples *something new.*

Finally three pm the workshop was over, before that we were given a paper to fill in our names, *we were about to get paid!* This was to be done as we walked out signing on the list and Ka-ching! Money in my pocket.

This was not enough, how could I prove my worth earning pennies. This was never going to make my uncles proud of me; they would give my mother hell for taking me out of S.A. I had to find another 'plan'. So I applied at the Hotel, I had experience from the three restaurants I worked at in South Africa; this place would be a piece of cake. The other bonus I thought I had was the manager, she was my neighbor and used to be my younger uncle's friend and her brother was my uncle and dad's friends. *Almost like family,* I thought. Still I took the chance, spoke to her, smiling just as I was taught in S.A and she seemed thrilled to see me. Asking me where I had been, I hated that question. I responded anyways. And the horror of all questions came *why did you come back?* I did not get what people saw in S.A that was so great. The place was not that special; it broke me, almost made me an addict, and almost killed me. In fact, it killed me; I died while I was in South Africa, Johannesburg. She smiled back at me and said *I will see you at home, do not worry I will try something out for you.* I left, full of confidence. I walked back home, it is quite a distance from the Hotel to my home; I walked. Forty minutes or was it an hour later I got home, with a dollar saved. I was going to use it on my first day of work, if she came through for me.

Told my mother the semi good news, she pulled me to the bedroom and started praying. Thanking God, this was it, we thought; my spirit guide had brought me out of the wilderness and guided me home. She, *the manager/neighbor* came; I took my CV to her place, easiest job search I thought. That was the last I saw of my CV and her. She ghosted me; I did not go to her house and ask after her, my pride could not let me. I felt my hopes shatter. Another attempt failed.

Chapter 33

I wrote to flush out my frustrations. I scribbled in my diary, poured out all my anger. Sometimes I would draw, under the alias of Aries Rage.
Someday I will get these sewn and have them on the runway I would say then chuckle to myself. I never stopped sending out CVs, and they never stopped not calling back. If only they sent a rejection letter, I would have gotten some closure out of it. The dreaded question never stopped coming, *what is your plan* and each time I had a different answer and soon enough I was starting to stop believing in my answers. I recall telling my youngest uncle that I was planning to make and sell shwamas and Kota's I had the experience so it was bound to be easy. *But with what money* the clothes business was drowning, people were not paying us and we could not use the rent money because some 'renovations' and 'wall painting' was in the works. We would sometimes sleep on scraps of food and I would curse on my spirit guide for the wrong call. I was seriously considering going back to South Africa. The only place I knew that could give me the job I needed. I could not prove my worth I had again failed.

I was a disappointment and felt that I deserved a crown.
The voices became louder, the dreams clearer and I still did not have a job. I found a group on Facebook with members who were like me. I was looking for answers and hopefully a job. They heard voices talking to them, they were down and out, and they wanted to tap out. Someone, one day posted on the group sharing an experience on OBE *out of body experience or astral projection.* I was curious; it could be something I wanted to do. Leave my body and never come back. That is what I had in mind.
I did it, guided by another member who soon became my spiritual mentor. He was just the person I needed in my life; he got me focused on meditation and not on ending my life. He kept me grounded. Helped me face my fears, *though there are fears I still need to work on.* I do not recommend being an only child it comes with a lot of emotional trauma. Do not get me wrong, it is not bad, not at all, but comes with a lot of yearning for validation. My mother gave me all the praise I could ever want but it was my uncles I needed to prove a point to, I wanted to hear them say they were proud of me.

The OBE experience was exhilarating, scary, but exciting.
I lay on my back, on the floor facing up as instructed. I said three chanting words, a mantra to keep me focused as I entered the astral plane. I chanted, repeatedly and I became one with the words. I was supposed to find my jump of point, a point in my mind where I can connect with when I want to stop projecting. It sounded easy in theory, but doing it was difficult. I could not stop my mind from talking; making plans, cancelling plans, and thinking of ways to validate myself in my uncle's eyes.
Let go of yourself when you find your jump off point. I had to let go of all the worries that floated in my head and focus. I struggled to find my jump off point at first, each time I

came close to it my mind thought of something that was not relevant to the meditation process and I was pulled out. I used that confusion that riddled my mind and I saw myself standing on the edge of what looked like a mountain, I remembered my mentor's words and leaped off.

When I jumped, I did not fall on my face instead I saw myself walking in a garden. It was serene, the green was luscious, very fertile, and it was welcoming. I continued walking and came to an old building; it had a rocky pavement that looked as if it was rained on. I entered through the door; it was slightly flung open as if someone was waiting for me. I found myself in what looked like a lobby of a hotel, I looked up and saw a high ceiling that was dome shaped, like the inside of some church in Rome I had seen on TV. My spiritual mentor had told me to ask the question that was important at this time; *who am I?* I did as instructed, and as if in an instant I started having flash backs of a life supposedly to be mine. I saw myself kneeling and surrounded by figures that had animal heads. I saw different animals, some were totems that I knew; I saw mine, the lion. It was standing amongst the others; I do not remember feeling afraid. Almost instantly, after seeing these figures, I turned and looked behind me and I saw the woman I had seen before; *the Priestess* dressed exactly like one of the Tarot cards I had drawn out while I was in S.A.

As I was about to go near her, I jolted up as if in fright. I saw the number four as I came to, and texted my spiritual mentor. He explained to me all that I had seen. It was nothing new that I had not heard. I was gifted and there was no running away from it.

Chapter 34

I got a call for an interview in town. The person on the other end told me to get there before ten. I had always been a punctual person, be it an hour early, or a day early. It was sometime in 2018, I came across a job call on Facebook; risky I know but had no choice. Green World was the company; they specialized in herbal medicines for chronic ailments such as cancer. They were looking for distributors. It was not im my field, but I figured I would learn something and be paid in the process. I arrived at the said location, an office in the second floor of the CABS building. It seemed legit, I texted my mother telling her that I had arrived, a habit I had brought with me from South Africa. *Of course, Zimbabwe was much safer than South Africa, but I had only spoken to these people online.* I don't own much of formal wear in my wardrobe so that day I had opted for the only long skirt I had then that had two slits running down my legs at the front and a white top I had borrowed from mum.

I remember ambling in the corridor, checking the door numbers, looking for the said office. I saw a swarm of people buzzing into the office I was looking for, they too were dressed in black and white others in green the company colors. As I entered, the chairs were not arranged as one would an office. It looked as if there was some kind of presentation waiting to be shown. The projector had already been set up, I thought I was lost or was late for the interview. I checked the picture and name of the person I was supposed to meet, I asked a friendly elderly woman that was, what I thought the usher. She directed me to a make shift office which they had divided from the main room. I saw the person I was supposed to meet; he was creepier in person than on the picture. Good thing there were about ten if not more people in the room. He told me they were about to do the presentation and that I should join in. I had not brought a notebook; neither did I have a pen, but the elderly woman came to my rescue. A note pad and a pen in hand I shoved myself in the corner, strategically, not to close to be picked as a participant if they needed any, and not too far to see the presentation.

It went on for about an hour maybe more. The more they explained the distributor position the more it sounded like a pyramid scheme. *Start in the bronze package and add two distributors under your name or sell to five customers you will be moved to the silver package, to move up to the platinum you need to have the two people under you to add two each and they do the same you will end up in the Gold package.* I tried scribbling down the steps as the presenter spoke brimming with confidence. She had moved into the gold package and she was being given a holiday incentive to Victoria Falls. *Nice!* I thought. A testimony from a member in the Harare branch said the lad was getting a house plus a holiday in China.

It sounded too good to be true, but they had the evidence, pictures to prove it. *It could be*

anyone I thought. They gave us lessons on the herbs they sold and tablets made from those herbs. I wondered how I was going to sell and get myself in the big league. I could feel that it was not the job for me, I had so much doubt and questioned every point I had written down. I waited until everyone else had left, leaving only the office owners rearranging the furniture. The nice elderly woman started calling me daughter, telling me that I needed to join them. *It is the most fulfilling job you can ever have!* She shrieked. I looked at her, stole a glimpse at the feet (a habit I had been accustomed to); her shoes had seen better days. They looked tired, as if their life had been sucked dry by some life-sucking beast. I went back to her face; she wore a smile, wider than a clown did. It seemed fake, below the happy chappy exterior, she was hurting; I could tell she wanted out but could not, and it was as if she wanted me to rescue her. I said my fare well to the man who had called me in for the interview and he offered to see me out.
He walked me to the rank, where I would get my ride home. As we walked, he talked about how he had benefited from the company. I looked at his feet; he had decent shoes on, *church shoes* I thought. In his chatter, it seemed as though he was begging me to join, just as that elderly woman was begging me; all I could sense from their begging was RUN!

He started texting me, I told him I was thinking about it; I was not. My spiritual instincts were telling me that it was not the job for me. He asked me out. *Lunch, he* said. I told him that I could not do that. *It was not professional,* I said. I had far more important things to deal with, like getting a job where I was not going to be hit on. He kept on pressing and I kept on evading, I ended up blocking him. It was the only way.

Chapter 35

I woke up one morning with words bustling in my head. As if it were following a certain pattern, they were not just meaningless words, they were almost poetic, and they were pushing to come out. I started to meditate on the words; this was definitely not my mind overthinking. I centered my breathing, and my mind. The noise stopped, I opened my eyes and wondered what was happening to me. I recall doing my chores, and a sudden urge to write forced its way as if it wanted to come out. I started reciting the mantra my Spiritual guide taught me. Then everything went blank, it was as if I zoned out. I then heard a voice, a familiar one; my spirit guide with an instruction that was as clear as day said, *you should start writing. Find yourself a book and write everything you hear from now on. I will guide you.* I wondered what these writings were going to help with. I wanted a job that was going to help me prove to my uncles that I was someone, proving my worth and giving me an identity. I did not see this writing gig giving me what I wanted.

I told my mom about the instruction I had received and without any second thought, she took the last dollar note that she had and told me to find a book and start writing. I hated that, it made me feel worse than I was already feeling. I did not like having to use the last money we had, especially if that money was going to help us in some other way. My mom did not want to hear any excuse I had to give. I went to a local shop and found a diary; it was big and had more than enough pages that could last me a while.
Then I started writing, drawing from my experience in South Africa, and spiritual experiences. It all came flowing like lava; word by word burning the exit of my brain, soon I had a collection of poems. I then started writing a story, had characters, plots and a setting. I titled it *Vimbai* at first*; and then considered the title a beautiful hell.* Effortlessly it flowed and so did questions of what I was going to do with it after I was done.

I got a job, finally!
My uncle (my father's youngest brother), got it for me. He spoke to his friend and former colleague who worked at a bank. It is funny how both my uncles played a role in getting me jobs. It did not help me get rid of my obsession of wanting to prove myself. I wanted something that I had done, by myself so that THEY would be genuinely proud of me. Steward bank was my new home away from home. I was employed as a brand ambassador, not as luxurious as it sounds, but after long excruciating walks under the burning sun or coldest winters we got paper rolling in our accounts. Our job description as the B.A.s was to find people and get them to open an account with the bank. With my new friends, now sisters *Beverly, Emily, and Sharon*, we would tear up the city one company after the other reaching places I never thought existed. We would have fun throughout chatting window-shopping and daydreaming, sometimes we would sit at the park under the big trees' shade. We did not have much, our paychecks were not as attractive as our title; but whatever meal we had was amazing. It must have been the love

amongst us.
Despite coming back home from work exhausted, I would tap away on my laptop. My mom would cheer me on, and push me to write even when I did not feel like writing. *I secretly think that she did not want me to be punished by my spirit guide.*

I finished my book, did not know what next. I sought help from Facebook, joined writer's groups, and dropped a question. You could call it a cry for help, *I have written a book what do I do now, how do I get people reading it?* Lucky for me the members were so friendly. They gave me the dos and don'ts of being an author. I was overwhelmed with information. I then got a message in my private inbox. Two publishers were interested in helping me, *but I have no money to publish* I told the one I felt much more akin to. She told me to send in my books to her email. I did it, A Beautiful Hell was published and the title became...

I became Aries Rage.
Even though I had escaped South Africa, the urge to escape some more overwhelmed me. I needed an identity; coming to Zimbabwe had not help me find one. I had emotions bottled up, emotions of anger, resentment, and disappointment boiling in the pit of my stomach. It was as if I had lost myself in South Africa and Zimbabwe hosted a body without a soul. I needed an outlet, and so I created an alter ego, one that was unapologetic, one that I could use to express all that was bottled up in me. Aries Rage became that outlet, and now that I had published two books, I had been exposed to a world of Poets and writers. I poured my pain in words, and they swooned over them. I got relief, not from the fact that they read my work, but because I had told someone other than my mother.

Aries Rage gave me a voice, which I had lost. I found myself; she was hidden underneath a massive pain. Two books became three and international recognition along with it, I was noticed; finally I was visible.
I had a title to my name, Elizabeth Taderera published author. It sounded like everything that I ever wanted. If only my father was alive to celebrate with me and tell me how proud, he was of me. It was all I ever wanted; of course, my mother said it every day, but a part of me wants to hear my father's voice and pat on my back from his hand.

A yearn that is stronger each day as I wake. As I await to hear his voice, I discover myself, and the gift that is within me accepting all that I AM...

Epilogue

Dear Liz

You have grown, tears do not flow as much right?
Remember when you wished to grow up and stop being a crybaby. That wasn't your fault, you just had a lot of hurt, pain, and anger trapped inside the little body of yours; you just didn't know how to deal with it. You used to say life is a roller coaster ride, you had never been on a real one, but you have enough experience to get you through on other rides. Your teary South African nights should have been bottled and your afternoon smiles framed, you might never see that smile again. I applaud you for that, smiling through your toughest times even though you say it was faked your true self knew it was not. I knew that somewhere inside of you was a strong girl waiting to break free.

You wanted to fit in so much that it almost affected your growth. It could have ruined you and turned you into something that you are not. I am glad that you now know that this is not a prerequisite, you are you and can never be like someone else or fit in anyone's jigsaw puzzle as you are your own piece. A unique one at that...
I wonder, have you ever seen a perfect gem? One without flaws; if you do find one please let me know. Do you get what I am trying to tell you here? No? Let me just tell you.
Nothing in this world, of yours is perfect, everything has flaws, and it is okay not to be perfect. I think it only makes you unique. So stop beating yourself up for not being the perfect version you think you can be. I know this will long and winding plea, but Liz seriously! You are only human. I cannot scream this loud enough, YOU ARE ONLY HUMAN! Moreover, you can never please all humans, so STOP trying to live up to other people's expectations. You should aim at making yourself happy with the decisions you

make. Do not make choices to make other people happy, if they are to be proud of you, it is because of the effort you put into doing it your way.
I know you find it hard, it beats you black and blue thinking that you have failed your family; just because you didn't take the path that they hoped you would, it doesn't mean that you failed, you just did what you thought was best for you.
LIFE IS A MAZE OF MISTAKES, JUST FIND YOUR WAY TO A STARTING POINT, AND CORRECT YOURSELF.

One other thing sweet Liz, you should embrace fear. I know its weird reading this, but really, fear is your best friend. It is the best teacher you can ever ask from life. You may ask why. Well she teaches you that not all things in life are scary. Look, when you are afraid of going on a roller coaster, what happens? You see other people having fun right and you wish you were one of them. However, what if you feel scared and you go anyway and something bad happens; what does fear teach us? It teaches you to listen; listening to your gut is the best thing that could ever happen to you. Follow your instincts, they never stray you, if you listen attentively. Just do not let fear control your life, learn from your past mistakes.

I am proud of you that you have managed to let some things out. You held out on some, but I am happy that you took the important path, the one of finding yourself. I hope you will keep yourself, the true identity that is you! A unique creature that does not need validation, you are here for a reason and NOT to be anyone's pawn. You have the tools to be your own master but be careful not to be a slave to your own weaknesses. These (weaknesses) are only there to make way for your strengths. This is not a parting message I am with you; I am you. Remember what I told you, YOU CAN ONLY FIND YOUR TRUE SELF ONCE YOU LET GO OF YOURSELF.

Yours with love,

***

I found my old self, in the crevices of my past wallowing
in hate and regret choking on meaningless apologies,
stumbling on failed dreams; still she held out her hand
knowing that somehow I will see her light.
She glowed, and became a lighthouse,
showed me a way to what I could be.

I found my old self,
trapped in a cold pit of despair nursing wounds inflicted by a past
that had a hopeful future.
I wiggled her out through the twist and turns she came out scathed with bruises and
scratches she became a mural of red and brown_ like a chestnut.

I found my old self, basking in hope's glory and wondered how she found peace
in so much noise. Her scars were Braille for the blind Oracle
who saw the way out, and gave me strength to carry
my worries_ I found them trivial. I became a warrior.
I became my own Hero.

I am.

END.

www.ingramcontent.com/pod-product-compliance
Lightning Source LLC
LaVergne TN
LVHW080043170826
845677LV00024B/1560
* 9 7 9 8 2 3 0 5 7 0 4 9 3 *